UTMOST
ONGOING

OSWALD CHAMBERS

UTMOST ONGOING

REFLECTIONS *on the* LEGACY OF

OSWALD CHAMBERS

Discovery House.
from Our Daily Bread Ministries

Interior design by Beth Shagene

ISBN: 978-1-62707-679-1

Printed in the United States of America

First printing in 2017

CONTENTS

INTRODUCTION

Every day tens of thousands of people read the same entry in *My Utmost for His Highest* by way of an app, an email, a website, or their own copy of the book. A college freshman breaks open the volume his grandparents gave him when he graduated high school. A businesswoman, commuting into the city, listens to *Utmost* on her phone. A young musician discusses the devotional with her mentor. A war reporter, embedded in an army unit, pulls *Utmost* from his inside flak jacket, where he keeps the book close to his heart. A president reads Oswald Chambers in the morning quiet before taking coffee to the first lady.[1]

My Utmost for His Highest has been in print for nearly a hundred years. What accounts for the book's continued appeal to people of all ages and stations in life? To attempt an answer to this question, one must look at individual stories of *Utmost*'s influence.

In *Utmost Ongoing*, you'll hear from scientists, doctors, musicians, pastors, a soldier, a CEO, and others, from young authors to established Christian teachers. They all share

---

1. Musician Joy Williams, formerly of The Civil Wars, from http://www
.crosswalk.com/11617768/; late NBC reporter David Bloom, from
http://ericmetaxas.com/writing/essays/david-bloom-1963-2003;
former president George W. Bush, from http://www.newsweek.com
/bush-and-god-132561.

their interactions with *My Utmost for His Highest*, describing how it has taught them, convicted them, encouraged them, and changed them. Their life experiences vary widely, but each is united by a love for God's truth as taught by Oswald Chambers.

You may not agree with all of the perspectives in this book. The contributors themselves, if gathered into one room, might not agree on exactly how the Christian life should be lived. But this is the beauty of Christian fellowship—Jesus bound us to one another and asked us to love, despite our differences. And in all probability, when we look closely we'll find more that unites us than divides us.

As you read this book, keep in mind that *My Utmost for His Highest* is available in two editions, "classic" and "updated." The original book released in England in 1927 and in the United States in 1935. In 1992, James Reimann published an updated edition, what he called a "translation" into modern language. Quotes in *Utmost Ongoing* are taken from the classic, original edition of *My Utmost for His Highest* unless the phrase "updated edition" follows.

The publisher wishes to thank Josh Thompson at Word Records for coordinating the musicians' participation in this book, and Amy Peterson for assistance in finding other contributors. Thanks also to the Oswald Chambers Publications Association, Ltd., for encouragement to pursue the book.

May the stories in the pages that follow lead you to a richer relationship with the God to whom Oswald Chambers gave his utmost.

—Discovery House

LINA ABUJAMRA

*God can never make us wine if we object
to the fingers He uses to crush us with.*
SEPTEMBER 30, "THE COMMISSION OF THE CALL"

Every significant and life-changing encounter I've had with the Lord has grown out of pain. I don't mean to sound melodramatic. I'm simply speaking the truth.

I was sixteen when I surrendered my life to Jesus. It was a typical night at a typical Christian camp, but for me there was nothing typical about that moment. God called me to follow Him and I said yes.

Somehow, I thought that that would be the end of my struggles with God. I thought that the rest of my life would be simple. Little did I know that saying yes to the Lord was actually the easiest step in following Jesus. The best, and the worst, was yet to come.

Growing up in Beirut, Lebanon, I had watched my mother clutch her Bible in the middle of the night, crying out to God in our improvised shelter, praying that we would make it through the bombing unharmed. But at other times, too, she spent hours on her knees.

As I got older I noticed that next to my mother's Bible

always lay a small book written by a man named Oswald Chambers. I figured that since my mom kept that book near her Bible, it must have been very important. At the time I didn't understand her attachment to *My Utmost for His Highest*, but once I began chasing after God and seeking materials to help me deepen my walk with Him, I gravitated to what I knew best. I got my own little version of *My Utmost*, and next to my Bible it became my closest companion.

At first I didn't really understand everything Chambers wrote. But I persevered in reading the book. Several years passed, and by the time I turned twenty-nine I'd caught the Oswald Chambers bug. My love affair with *My Utmost for His Highest* couldn't have come at a better time.

That year I had just begun my pediatric emergency medicine fellowship in a new town where I knew no one. It was the same year that I had overcome a great personal disappointment that broke my heart and shattered my dreams. It was also the year in which I started attending a new church, and God had allowed me to start teaching His Word to anyone brave enough to show up to the ladies Sunday school class. This was the year that I started seeing God's Word with fresh eyes. It was the year I fell more deeply in love with Jesus than ever.

So it was around that time that I really started seeking the Lord, asking Him about His plans for my life. On January 31, 2001, while reading *My Utmost*, I came across a phrase from Romans 1:1, "separated unto the Gospel." I knew in that moment and without a doubt that God was calling me to proclaim the gospel in full-time vocational ministry. Oswald Chambers had inadvertently (or providentially) become a part of my vocational calling, and I couldn't have chosen a better mentor and friend.

Once again, though, I found that I had naively believed

that saying yes to God's call would be the hardest part of my journey with Jesus, that somehow the rest would be simple. It wasn't. The path that followed would lead me through the wilderness, stripped of my comforts and at times uncertain of the future. Until that point I still had not fully grasped that, in God's economy, pain is the currency for growth. But slowly, even though my path was becoming more difficult, I was learning to be more certain of my God.

John Piper has written that books don't change people, paragraphs do—sometimes even sentences. In the early years of my calling, on one particular September 30, I read in *My Utmost* a sentence that would indelibly leave its mark on my life, changing me forever: "God can never make us wine if we object to the fingers He uses to crush us with."

The first time I read those words, I resisted them. What kind of God would be willing to do that to His children? I didn't like the idea of being squeezed, and certainly not by my loving heavenly Father. Hadn't I committed to following Jesus? Hadn't I obeyed Him to the best of my abilities? Having done my part, wouldn't God do *His* and subsequently bless me?

I had yet to understand that a God who would bless us is a God who is first willing to break us. Psalm 66:10–12 (ESV) says, "For you, O God, have tested us; you have tried us as silver is tried. You brought us into the net; you laid a crushing burden on our backs; you let men ride over our heads; we went through fire and through water; yet you have brought us out to a place of abundance." The psalmist understood that God's purpose in our pain is always to perfect us. While God allows us to go through the fire, He remains near enough to make sure we come out of the fire unharmed.

Our heavenly Father is good. His ways are always perfect. He is willing to crush us, but He does it lovingly and only in order to benefit us. He takes what is broken and restores it for His use. He gives beauty for ashes and turns mourning into dancing.

Starting in the Old Testament and running all the way through Revelation, we see story after story of men and women who were stripped for God's glory. They were stripped of their homes and their families. They were stripped of their lives and safety. They were stripped of their reputations and possessions. And they were raised to shine brightly in a dark world desperate for the bright light of Jesus.

These men and women came to God with great expectation and hope, ceding their rights to themselves. They expected relief. They expected deliverance. What they often missed—what I often miss—is that God's deliverance always starts with Him stripping His followers of things that must go. His way slowly transforms us into vessels fit to be used for His purposes alone.

In 1915, Oswald Chambers had published only limited material and was relatively unknown. Though he was much loved in his circles, as a traveling evangelist and the principal of his own Bible college in London, the onset of what we know as World War I stirred him to serve God in a different way. Oswald Chambers became a chaplain to British troops serving in Egypt.

Two years later, still in the desert with the soldiers, Oswald had a routine and simple surgery—an appendectomy. No one could have predicted that his life would end from postoperative complications. No one expected that this rising star for God, this warrior for the kingdom, would finish his course at the age of forty-three.

When I first learned about Oswald Chambers's death, I was bitterly disappointed. Why would God crush this man's life in such a mundane way? An appendectomy? It seemed senseless and cruel. Yet God's ways never cease to amaze me, as it was Oswald himself who had uttered the very words that taught me God's chosen process for perfecting and using people: "God can never make us wine if we object to the fingers He uses to crush us with."

If we are to be made wine, we must be willing to submit to God's squeezing fingers. It was through Chambers's death that wine—and such fine, lasting wine—was made. It was his death that led to the compilation of *My Utmost for His Highest*.

Today more than 13 million copies of *Utmost* have been sold. It's been translated into dozens of languages and changed millions of people's lives—including mine. No friend in this world has walked so closely with me, through the highs and lows of my calling, as these words of Oswald Chambers have.

When I said yes to God's call, I had anticipated great victories and a life of ease. I didn't yet understand that when a person answers the Savior's call, by far the best decision in the world, it is also the hardest. After all, it means following the example of the One who was stripped for our sake.

The pressure of the Father's fingers makes a man or woman fit for Christ. It is this crushing that allows greater usefulness for the King. It is the stripping process that distinguishes the true saint from the casual observer. And it is the pain that allows us to finally reach the place of abundance in Christ.

Every significant and life-changing encounter I've had with God has grown out of pain. As Oswald so wisely explained: "Grapes become wine only when they have been squeezed. . . . Keep right with God and let Him do what He likes, and you will find that He is producing the kind of bread and wine that will benefit His other children."

Oswald Chambers's words continue to benefit God's children today. As he submitted to God's crushing fingers, he became the kind of bread and wine that people dream of tasting. I owe the man a debt of gratitude—he helped me to experience a life radically changed by the crushing fingers of a faithful and loving heavenly Father.

Lina Abujamra is an author, speaker, and pediatric emergency room doctor who loves Jesus. Although she enjoys caring for kids in the ER, her first passion is to tell others about Jesus and the love He has for them. Lina was born and raised in Beirut, Lebanon, and now calls Chicago home. She has written three books—*Thrive: The Single Life as God Intended, Stripped: When God's Call Turns from Yes to Why Me?* and *Resolved: 10 Ways to Stand Strong and Live What You Believe.*

HAROLD MYRA

What was the joy that Jesus had? . . . the joy
of doing that which His Father sent Him to do.
"I delight to do Thy will." . . . Be rightly
related to God, find your joy there, and out
of you will flow rivers of living water.
AUGUST 31, "MY JOY . . . YOUR JOY"

In this quote, Oswald Chambers speaks of joy and delight—
but in our era of constant anxiety, those are not very common
experiences. Every day we see dynamic videos of disasters
around the globe, with dire predictions of worse things to
come. Family troubles seem insoluble. Leaders fail to lead,
and injustices spread. Instead of joy, we may well feel help-
lessness. Yet Jesus, surrounded by terrible injustice and trouble in His world, experienced delight because of His unique
bond with His Father.

The thing that puts troubles into perspective, says Chambers, is being in tune with the Father. *Joy . . . the Father . . .*
obedience . . . rivers of living water. They are all connected.

As I ponder the tremendous international impact of
Utmost, I'm reminded of Jesus's observation that a bit of yeast
works its way through a lump of dough (Luke 13:21). A daily

dose of Chambers, in leader after leader all over the world, has blessed many an enterprise, ministry, and community. Leaders facing rugged challenges but tenaciously living by *Utmost*'s stringent truths have stayed purposeful and faithful.

One such leader was the beloved pastor Richard Halverson, who became chaplain of the United States Senate. He started reading *Utmost* early in his life and never stopped dipping into it daily. "Through the years," he wrote, "Chambers has kept me on course by bringing me back to Jesus. Believing Jesus, not just believing my beliefs about Jesus, is basic."

It's amazing to me how many leaders, including those writing in this book, have found *Utmost* essential—for instance, my mentor Fred Smith, a successful businessman and lay leader. Fred had a sharp eye for hypocrisy, and because he saw human nature so clearly, he could easily have lapsed into cynicism. Yet long ago I concluded Fred's reading of Chambers, day after day, year after year, had a marvelous effect on him. He would mention "aha moments" from *Utmost*. He drew from its stark realism, and he saw in Jesus what Chambers observed—that Jesus had no illusions about what was in the human heart, though He was never cynical.

That sort of redemptive realism is what we aimed for in *Christianity Today*'s news stories, when we had to report sobering facts about the misdeeds of Christians. Their failures in no way invalidated the gospel.

"We live by God's surprises": at Christianity Today International (CTI), we took that as a corporate motto for all our magazines. It's a phrase resonant with Chambers's themes. He said that being born again of the Spirit is "as mysterious as the wind, as surprising as God Himself . . . a perennial, perpetual and eternal beginning, a freshness all the time in thinking and in talking and in living, the continual surprise of the life of God" (January 20).

We knew that God's surprises weren't all warm and fuzzy, but sometimes "mysterious" . . . and sometimes extremely difficult. Chambers cautions, "Do not look for God to come in any particular way, but *look for Him*. . . . The great lesson to learn is that at any minute He may break in. . . . Always be in a state of expectancy" (January 25).

At CTI, we emphasized an expectancy for God to work through prayer—while remaining open to whatever would come. *Utmost* put that in painful perspective: "We must never put our dreams of success as God's purpose for us; His purpose may be exactly the opposite" (July 28).

Whoa! What was Chambers saying about all our hard work, and our dreams and our prayers? Well, at CTI all of us knew that in any ministry or business, failure is as frequent as success—and Chambers captured the dynamic: "What is my dream of God's purpose? His purpose is that I depend on Him and on His power now. . . . His end is the process—that I see Him walking on the waves, no shore in sight, no success, no goal, just the absolute certainty that it is all right because I see him walking on the sea" (July 28).

Many of us took Chambers's word picture personally, especially when he added, "God's end is to enable me to see that He can walk on the chaos of my life just now" (July 28).

Chaos? If we're alive, we experience failures, grief, and yes, even personal chaos. Yet as we turn to God when bad things happen, we find meaning and opportunity to minister to others.

Most of us have preconceived ideas about what *should* happen if we stay faithful and work hard. In our celebrity culture, some feel the need to be recognized. We all want to contribute, and contribute largely if possible. But Chambers punctures balloons: "It is inbred in us that we have to do exceptional things for God; but we have not. We have to be exceptional in the ordinary things, to be holy in mean streets, among mean people, and this is not learned in five minutes" (October 21).

Not learned quickly indeed! Life slaps us in the face. Mean people—both in the sense of the disagreeable and in Chambers's primary usage, that of the average or ordinary— bring us down. *Utmost* doesn't dodge life's raw realities; its honesty is one reason for its great power. "The Christian life is gloriously difficult," Chambers tells us, "but the difficulty of it does not make us faint and cave in, it rouses us up to overcome. . . . Thank God He does give us difficult things to do! His salvation is a glad thing, but it is also a heroic, holy thing. It tests us for all we are worth" (July 7).

When I remember this challenge of being tested, I think of my son Rick. In high school he was a mediocre student— until he started playing football. He loved the game and, despite its roughness, gave it his all. Rick started living the way he played football, pushing himself for better grades, taking life's hits and rising again and again. In football and in life, painful blows keep coming; everyone gets tested. In that context Chambers declares, "God's grace turns out men and women with a strong family likeness to Jesus Christ, not milksops" (July 7). None of us want to be milksops!

Life is difficult. It's easy to wilt when the big bruisers trample us . . . or grief invades our lives. At CTI a beloved colleague with small children was diagnosed with terminal cancer. Sorrow permeated our halls; it felt tragically wrong! Yet during a prayer time our cancer-stricken colleague quoted the Virgin Mary's response to the angel who told her she would become pregnant with Jesus: "Let it be to me according to your word" (Luke 1:38 ESV).

Our colleague died, but we were buoyed by his steadfast faith. Over the years in our publishing ministry we lost other dear men and women, and each time it seemed contrary to what a loving God should want for His children. Yet Chambers envisions ways such adversity teaches us to walk by faith: "What a revelation it is to know that sorrow and bereavement and suffering are the clouds that come along with God!" (July 29).

Throughout our lives, we are tested—often severely—to keep faith vibrant. I like Chambers's image of our being like surfers: big waves threaten to overwhelm the ordinary swimmer, but they bring joy to the surfer who rides them.

Yet the image with the strongest personal resonance, and one to which *Utmost* returns often, is that of children with their heavenly Father. We may carry large responsibilities and achieve good things, but above all, we must align ourselves with the Father's will. When I'm tempted to see my work as more important than others', I can smile at this from Chambers: "Beware of posing as a profound person; God became a Baby" (November 22). He contrasts our self-centeredness with "the robust, simple life of the child of God" (June 21). And he declares, "What a splendid audacity a childlike child has" (August 28).

The mysterious, often difficult, surprises of life keep coming, and Oswald Chambers says that an awareness of God at work in them gives us an "attitude of child-wonder" (March 29). It's telling that Chambers, in his personal life, loved playing with children!

In our anxieties and the pressures of life, how do we sense child-wonder? It starts with prayer, and as publisher of *Christianity Today* I was intrigued by this in *Utmost*: "Prayer does not fit us for the greater works; prayer *is* the greater work" (October 17).

Prayer is where battles and victories are fought. That's why our team at CTI, facing challenges that could have sunk the ministry, regularly prayed together. We saw each other as servants of God and of each other. We placed on each manager's desk a sculpture of Jesus washing the feet of Peter.

Prayer helped us not to take ourselves too seriously. It was encouraging in the hallways to hear so much laughter coming from offices and at the coffee station. Children secure in the love of their Father can laugh. They can find joy and delight even in an anxious world.

Harold Myra served as CEO of Christianity Today International for thirty-two years. Under his leadership, the organization grew from one magazine to a communications company with a dozen magazines, copublished books, and a major Internet ministry. Author of numerous books and hundreds of magazine articles, Myra has taught writing and publishing at the Wheaton College Graduate School in Illinois. Harold and his wife, Jeanette, are the parents of six children and grandparents of nine. They reside in Wheaton, Illinois.

BLANCA

If it is an impossibility,
it is the thing we have to ask.
FEBRUARY 29, "WHAT DO YOU WANT
THE LORD TO DO FOR YOU?"

"What do you want me to do for you?" (Luke 18:41).

I remember reading these words of Jesus and feeling like I'd been punched right in the heart. Real, honest truth will do that to you. It's like a light being directed into the darkest corner of that little area in your life that no one else has seen.

How many times have I second-guessed God and His promises? How many times have I tried to convince myself of something rather than just dive in with childlike faith? How many times have I allowed my personal failure to overshadow God's character and cloud my confidence of Him as almighty?

I've dealt with fear and doubt for most of my life, so I think that's why Chambers's February 29 devotional hits me so directly and personally. It's easy for me to err on the side of caution and common sense. Our flesh enjoys figuring things out, gathering up all the answers, and keeping uncomfortable things at a comfortable distance. We desire a map before we take the next step.

For many years, I mastered the art of protecting my heart from disappointment, all the while plastering a smile on my face to convince others that everything was just fine. I would rehearse an outcome in my head before I even asked God for His help. For so long I was reluctant to approach Him with boldness and confidence.

We tend to paint a portrait of God based on the encounters we have had with other people. The way I've communicated with Him proves this. Yet, in His infinite mercy, God doesn't require us to have everything figured out before we tell Him our issues. That just isn't how He works. I'm realizing more and more that God is in the business of completing impossibilities. Key word: *completing*. He doesn't just attempt, He perfects.

The updated edition of *My Utmost* adds emphasis to the February 29 quote above: "If it is an impossibility, it is the *very* thing for which we have to ask." Really think about that for a moment: whenever we face a situation that is outside our strength and control, we have a direct indication of what we should be praying about. You see, this is one of the fundamental parts of our faith walk. The deeper we go in our relationship with God, the more we learn His character. And the more we learn His character, the more we believe He is who He says He is and that He'll do what he says He'll do.

My past year has been a difficult one. It has been full of obstacles too big for me to overcome, one in particular being my mom's battle with terminal cancer. The thought of losing someone who means so much to me has shaken my faith to the core. And fear likes to creep in when these things happen—fear of the unknown, fear of what's to come, fear of God not coming through in the way we desire.

I've noticed in these times of discomfort, or as Oswald Chambers would say, "disturbances," how easy it is to think the worst, to believe the problems confronting me are scary, fixed realities with no chance of change.

It is easy to accept what is already in front of you, but much more difficult to believe what you cannot see . . . yet. The *very* thing I want to ask God to do for me is the one thing I don't request, for fear of Him not coming through. It's almost as if my not asking at all will save my perception of God.

Now hear me clearly when I say this: I don't believe, and neither does Chambers, that God is some sort of genie ready to grant every wish at our command and on our schedule. The fundamental truth Chambers is trying to portray is that everything in life must flow from a deep relationship with Jesus. In His Word, the Lord gave us the example that He is the vine and we are the branches. Without Him, we can do absolutely nothing. It isn't enough to know *about* Jesus, we must actually know Him . . . personally.

I've had to shift my posture in many ways to understand this truth. I've had to change my perspective on how I approach challenges to have a clearer picture of who God is, what He desires, and what I choose to believe of Him. I don't want to fearfully and anxiously ask God to heal my mother, and then hope—with my fingers crossed—that He delivers.

No, I refuse to allow any type of doubt and unbelief to plant seeds of fear when I speak to my heavenly Father. Instead I want to be so close to His heart that it's as if I can already anticipate His next move. I want to describe my relationship with God just as a husband and wife who know each other like no one else does: when He speaks, I know His voice; when He smiles, I feel His kindness; when He holds me, I am familiar with His comfort. That, to me, is what truly matters more than anything in this world.

My favorite quote is toward the end of this incredible

devotional: "We find faith by not only believing what Jesus says, but, even more, by trusting Jesus Himself. If we only look at what He says, we will never believe. Once we *see* Jesus, the impossible things He does in our lives become as natural as breathing" (updated edition, emphasis mine).

How beautiful is this picture he's painted for us? To not only take God at His Word, but to actually *see* Him working in our lives. This is a key reason God sent us His Son—to *show* us who He is.

I know that God's timing can sometimes seem "off" from our own. We set many expectations without ever consulting Him. Then we become disappointed when things don't go the way we anticipated. But one thing I have come to know very well: God does more in our waiting than we could ever do in all our striving.

God is a healer, a redeemer, a restorer—and nothing is impossible for Him to perfect and complete. It's easy to allow challenges to push us away from God, but I feel compelled now more than ever to do the opposite. I want to be so close in my relationship with God that I naturally see Him moving and working on my behalf.

Over time, I have learned that if we allow ourselves to indulge the habit of fearing the unknown, we will ultimately stagnate within our comfort zones. I read through the Bible and cannot help but notice circumstance after circumstance where Jesus challenged the faith of those He loved. Did you catch that? He challenged the *faith* of those He loved. Look at Peter, for example. He declared Jesus was Lord, walked on water to Him, then found himself sinking due to fear. Peter boldly declared that he would follow Jesus to the death, then a few days later denied he even knew the Lord.

Out of love, Jesus challenged Peter's faith, knowing it would make Peter stronger in the end. And if Jesus challenged

Peter, we'd better believe He will challenge *us* too. It is His way of preparing us for the days ahead.

When I look back upon my life, I know this is true. I have tasted defeat, and I have lived in the victory. I have seen many things that I haven't understood, often questioning why God would have allowed some things to transpire—but then I reminded myself of His faithfulness. Has He ever allowed the righteous to be forsaken? The Bible says not even once (Psalm 37:25). God's track record is perfect.

He has fulfilled countless impossibilities. So when I fear to approach Him with certain requests, I am just trying to hide myself from Him. But we were never intended to shy away from God when we are in need—we were meant to thrive in His limitless measures of grace!

"If it is an impossibility,
it is the thing we have to ask."

In recent years, Blanca got married, gave birth to a son, and launched a solo singing career outside of Group 1 Crew, with whom she had spent her entire professional life. In her self-titled release, Blanca dared to confront parts of herself that had been hidden from view. After addressing family challenges, career questions, and personal fears, she says her dreams are starting to come true. "I am at a point where I'm ready to completely be me," she says. "No more waiting. No more excuses."

CAROL KENT

Readiness means a right relationship to God and a knowledge of where we are. . . . Readiness for God means that we are ready to do the tiniest little thing or the great big thing, it makes no difference. . . . A ready person never needs to get ready. . . . The burning bush is a symbol of everything that surrounds the ready soul, it is ablaze with the presence of God.
APRIL 18, "READINESS"

It was a season of sadness. Following two and a half years and seven postponements of my son's trial, he was convicted of first-degree murder and sentenced to life in prison, without the possibility of parole.[2] Wallowing in grief and self-pity, I began spending less time in the Bible and even less time in prayer. My son, a US Naval Academy graduate, had done the unthinkable: he shot and killed his wife's first husband. There could be no do-overs. There could be no happy ending.

My husband and I were devastated—with the losses of the victim's family, the losses of our son and his family, and with our own losses. Following our son's conviction, we knew we

---

2. You can read the whole story in *When I Lay My Isaac Down* (NavPress, 2004).

would spend every weekend standing in line, usually for two hours, to get through the screening at a maximum-security prison just to visit him.

We could carry no cell phones or other electronic devices, books or games—only a car key, a driver's license, our official visitation card, and up to fifty dollars in cash for food from the vending machines. My husband and I were used to multitasking, with a long to-do list and deadlines for getting important things done. Waiting in line with other prison families did not feel productive. It didn't feel worthwhile. It felt as if the system was designed to punish the families along with their incarcerated loved ones. The longer I stood in those lines, the more irritated, upset, and angry I became. Where was God in the middle of these circumstances?

Then one day I saw my burning bush—my marker moment—as I had read about in the updated edition of *My Utmost*: "The burning bush is a symbol of everything that surrounds the person who is ready, and it is on fire with the presence of God Himself." It came through my husband's response to the same experience.

Gene talked to the children of inmates who were at the prison to visit their incarcerated fathers, entertaining them while they waited. I saw the relief and appreciation on the faces of their mothers. He introduced me to a teacher who was there to visit her husband, and I listened as she shared her story. We had something in common—a loved one on the "inside"—and we received strength from each other. I saw Gene take extra dollar bills out of his pocket for the mother of five small children, and I overheard him say, "Here's some help with food money for your kids while you're at the prison today."

Then came the day that I saw a woman turned away at the front of the line for wearing a sleeveless blouse—that was against prison visitation regulations. She had already driven several hours to the prison, then waited in a long line. As she left the entrance to drive to the nearest store—over twenty miles away—she was sobbing. I was so focused on her that I didn't immediately notice Gene leaving my side and walking back to our car in the parking lot. Reaching into our trunk, he pulled out a black T-shirt, then carried it over to the woman. I heard him say, "Just put this on and go to the front of the line. Have a wonderful visit with your loved one. It's my gift to you." Slipping the T-shirt over her head, she went back in and passed inspection.

Gene returned to me in the line, and I said, "So that's what's been happening to your black T-shirts." He smiled, looked down, and said, "It's my ministry."[3]

Time passed, and I began to identify what it meant for *me* to be in a mode of "readiness." My circumstances didn't change. My son's sentence did not get shorter. The security lines did not diminish. But I slowly began to realize that readiness to serve God in my situation had to begin with a right relationship to Him. I began spending time in the Word again and I asked God to speak to me through what I was reading. I started praying boldly, asking Him to nudge me with action steps to take in a situation that was going to last for the rest of my life. (According to Florida law, my son has a "toe tag sentence": he will only leave a state penitentiary when he has a tag on his toe—after he's passed away.)

I remembered reading in *My Utmost*, "Readiness for God means that we are prepared to do the smallest thing or the largest thing—it makes no difference." Conviction enveloped me. I had always been quick to do what felt like the "big

3. Read more about this experience and many others in *Waiting Together* (Discovery House, 2016).

things" for God—speaking, writing books, or challenging participants at a leadership conference. That felt like important work that deserved my time. But what would it look like for me, the mother of a prisoner with a life sentence, to do "the smallest thing"?

My attitude and my outlook began to change. I came to understand that "the smallest thing" in my view is often "the largest thing" in God's eyes. Before I left for prison visitation, I prayed, "Lord, help me to have a divine encounter with one of the families of inmates today." As I approached the prison driveway, I began praying with authority, "Father, may your presence be felt all over the prison today—throughout the cells where the inmates live, in the prison chapel, in the chow hall, in the visitation room, and among the people waiting in line to see their fathers, husbands, and friends today."

My circumstances didn't change, but I slowly began to anticipate what God would do as He opened doors for me— doors to personal encounters with people in the long line outside the building, as well as inside the prison once we all made it through the intake process.

Oswald Chambers said, "Be ready for the sudden surprise visits of God." Once Gene and I began talking to other prison families, hearing their questions and needs, we realized that our role in a public speaking and writing ministry could raise awareness and funds for them. God surprised us by making very clear what we could do to help, so we brainstormed with our son about the needs—of the inmates themselves and their families on the outside—and launched the non-profit organization Speak Up for Hope. We read Proverbs 31:8–9 and knew God was speaking to us about providing tangible assistance: "Speak up for those who cannot speak for themselves, for the rights of all who are destitute. Speak up and judge fairly; defend the rights of the poor and needy."

Our hearts had already been challenged by Chambers's call to be "there and ready. Whenever any duty presents itself, we hear God's voice as our Lord heard His Father's voice, and we are ready for it. . . . He can put us wherever He wants, in pleasant duties or in menial ones, because our union with Him is the same as His union with the Father."

Apart from my son's arrest and the unexpected journey that followed, I probably would not have chosen a ministry to inmates and their families as part of my life's work. However, I know now that this work is "on fire with the presence of God"—and I wouldn't trade it for anything. I long to be ready for action every time He reveals a need. I want to respond like Moses did. "God called to him . . . And Moses said, 'Here I am'" (Exodus 3:4).

 Carol Kent is an international speaker and best-selling author. With vulnerable openness, irrepressible hope, restored joy, and a sense of humor, she directs people to choices based on God's truth. "When God writes your story," she says, "you will be in for the adventure of a lifetime!" In addition to retreat and conference speaking, Carol annually directs the Speak Up Conference, training Christians in writing and speaking skills. She and her husband, Gene, run the ministry Speak Up for Hope (SpeakUpForHope.org), which seeks to encourage prisoners and their families. Carol can be found online at CarolKent.org.

JEREMY WRITEBOL

God called Jesus Christ to what seemed unmitigated
disaster. Jesus Christ called His disciples to see Him
put to death; He led every one of them to the place
where their hearts were broken. Jesus Christ's life was
an absolute failure from every standpoint but God's.
But what seemed failure from man's standpoint
was a tremendous triumph from God's, because
God's purpose is never man's purpose.
AUGUST 5, "THE BAFFLING CALL OF GOD"

August 5, 2014, was the darkest Tuesday of my life—my
mother, critically ill with the Ebola virus, was returning from
Liberia to the United States for treatment that we hoped
would save her life.

The previous ten days had been a whirlwind of emotion.
On July 26, my father had called late in the evening from
Monrovia to say that mom had contracted the disease. She
was serving as a nurse's assistant in the isolation unit of a mission organization hospital when she became ill. Since Ebola
was becoming epidemic in West Africa, international news
media quickly inundated us with requests for information
regarding my mother's condition and the family's response.

I had placed it in my mind that mom would—like so many overseas missionaries before her—lose her life to a foreign disease. We'd been told there was no possibility of transport from the small house where she was being isolated to a first-world medical facility capable of better fighting the virus.

So it was a great surprise when we learned that she would be medically evacuated to Emory University Hospital in Atlanta, Georgia. She was due to arrive on August 5.

As my father and I spoke during the time between mom's diagnosis and her transport and arrival in Atlanta, he shared how timely and encouraging Oswald Chambers's devotional had been to him. He would read *My Utmost* outside the bed-room window of the house where my mother was growing more and more ill, and it would sustain his heart through the gravity of the situation. When my brother and I arrived in Atlanta we too began to read Chambers's meditations along with some close friends. On the morning of August 5, as we awaited mom's nationally televised arrival and transport to Emory, we read in *My Utmost* "The Baffling Call of God."

Confident of God's call on my parents to serve Him in Africa, I was baffled by what they were enduring for the sake of the needy there. Furthermore, as I dealt with my own weary and broken heart, I was baffled at what God was doing in my own life. None of it made sense. It all seemed like failure—and the conclusion of the matter would be death. I could relate to the disciples when they heard about Jesus's mission to go to the cross: "They understood none of these things" (Luke 18:34 ESV).

We live in a cause-and-effect world, so trials and suf-fering bear down on us in ways we would never imagine. We desire—we try to insist on—lives that are clear-cut and explainable. We hate it when circumstances that we cannot control threaten our comfort and security. When hardships, suffering, and trials hit our lives, our faith can be jolted deeply. It's not uncommon for sufferers to bellow out to God, "Why?" And yet Jesus "led every one of [His disciples] to the place where their hearts were broken."

Suffering feels like failure, like complete and utter defeat. The world calls it foolish.

From a certain perspective Jesus's life looks a lot like this. As He left His family and carpentry trade at the age of thirty to begin an itinerant preaching ministry, He confused His family. They heard the reports of His ministry and miracles and concluded, "He is out of his mind" (Mark 3:21). He labored for the kingdom of God without a place to lay His head or call home (Luke 9:58). His teaching became difficult to understand, and the number of those who followed Him dwindled (John 6:66). As He confronted the religious establishment, He created powerful enemies who sought to have Him killed (Matthew 26:59). One of His own friends and followers betrayed Him for a small sum of money. He was slandered, beaten, abused, mocked, rejected, unjustly tried, and ultimately executed as a criminal, in shame and disgrace. The cross is foolishness if the "savior of the world" hangs dead upon it.

Yet, from another perspective—the biblical one—we can see our sufferings in another light. The apostle Paul called the cross the wisdom and power of God. He saw from God's standpoint a "tremendous triumph." Through the suffering and death of Jesus we have one who can stand in our place for our sins—and take them away. We have one who can mediate on our behalf and reconcile us to God. We have one who, by laying down His own life, won righteousness, peace, and life for us. "God made him who had no sin to be sin for us, so that in him we might become the righteousness of God" (2 Corinthians 5:21).

Following the utter defeat of the cross, the powerful resurrection of Jesus on the third day verified, vindicated, and
validated all the suffering He endured for our sake. "But
when Christ had offered for all time a single sacrifice for sins,
he sat down at the right hand of God, waiting from that time
until his enemies should be made a footstool for his feet. For
by a single offering he has perfected for all time those who
are being sanctified" (Hebrews 10:12–14 ESV).

This leads us back to our own trials. The Scriptures show
us that we should not be surprised by "the fiery ordeal"
(1 Peter 4:12). The Christian life is one that includes persecution (2 Timothy 3:12). We can expect difficulty and trials
as marks of discipline from the hand of a heavenly Father
who loves us and longs for us to be mature and complete
(James 1:2–4, Hebrews 12:5–11). Suffering is a mark of the
Christian life. Still, like so many in the world today, we want
to know the reason behind it.

But the gospel allows us to move ahead without having all
the answers, without knowing perfectly the purposes of God.
This doesn't mean that we can't ask the question or ponder
the big picture. We simply become, as Chambers states, "less
inclined to say—'Now why did God allow this and that?'"

If we see the goodness of God in the seemingly foolish
decision to send His Son to die on our behalf, then we can
embrace His call to what may feel like an "unmitigated disaster" in our own lives.

This is what the whole of faith truly boils down to: Can
I trust God? If we affirm that God is trustworthy and does
all things for His glory and our good then we can live with
an unparalleled freedom to receive both the triumphs and
the trials of life from His gracious hand. If all things work
together for the good of those who love God and are called

according to His purpose (Romans 8:28), then we are liberated from having to hold all the answers in our own hands.

The baffling call of God, although it can bewilder us, is ultimately a safe and rewarding call. It's a release from the ever-present desire to control and maintain all things by our own power. It means that I can be a child, safe in the hands of an omnipotent and gracious God, and He will lead me through the valley of the shadow of death (Psalm 23:4). Whatever God may have planned for my future—whatever He may call you to walk through—He is working out His purposes.

As the air ambulance carrying my mother landed at Dobbins Air Reserve Base outside Atlanta on August 5, I could only wonder at the baffling call of God. The aims of God's work and call in the life of my family were not clear. The anguish and turmoil of our hearts swelled as we became a public spectacle of suffering. My parents' mission to Liberia looked like an utter failure.

And yet, in God's hands and by His power, we could trust His great purposes. As a child of God I could cling to His mercy and ask for His grace in my pain. I could trust "the wits and the wisdom" of God, to use Chambers's phrase, that ultimately everything would be okay—even if that meant my mother's death.

I could even trust God's baffling call when mom's health made an incredible turn for the better. I could rest with joy when God healed her of the terrible Ebola virus. I could trust His providence when He called my parents back to Liberia—back to the mission—even when others might argue the cost was too great.

I can walk with a leisureliness of faith—because what looks like failure to the world is, from God's perspective, the fragrance of life.

 Jeremy Writebol is the lead campus pastor of Woodside Bible Church in Plymouth, Michigan, and executive director of Gospel-Centered Discipleship (GCDiscipleship.com). A graduate of Moody Bible Institute (B.A.) and a pastor for over fifteen years, Jeremy is committed to the advance of the gospel in every area of life. He is an author and contributor to several books and publications. You can find him regularly enjoying his family, a good cup of coffee, and a San Francisco Giants baseball game.

LORE FERGUSON WILBERT

*Growth in grace is measured not by the fact that
you have not gone back, but that you have an insight
into where you are spiritually; you have heard
God say "Come up higher," not to you personally,
but to the insight of your character.*

MARCH 27, "VISION BY PERSONAL CHARACTER"

It could be said of my spiritual life that it has been one long game of "step on the crack, break your mother's back; step on the line, break your daddy's spine."

Sound childish? It is. I have played darts, puzzles, and hide-and-seek with the God of the universe for almost all my life. I missed every bull's-eye, lost the puzzle pieces, and sought a God who seemed to do all the hiding while I was left looking around every corner, under every rock, through every open door and closed window. My life, too often, was built on clichés.

When I was in my late teens, two important things happened in my spiritual life. The first is that a respected professor in Bible school gave me a leather-bound copy of Scripture—my first—and the second is that inside the front cover I wrote these words of Oswald Chambers: "Growth in grace is measured not by the fact that you have not gone back, but that you have an insight into where you are spiritually; you have heard God say 'Come up higher,' not to you personally, but to the insight of your character."

The words were scrawled from the March 27 entry in *My Utmost for His Highest*. I had little understanding of doctrine, theology, or the path ahead of me, but I understood that those words meant something to me that day—and they would mean something to me for many days to come.

I was a sinner of the most blatant kind, which is why I say my life was built on clichés. I was the good kid who did bad things, and the bad kid who tried to do good things. I thought myself a saint and found myself a slave to the worst choices. In terms of "going back," I went seventy-five steps in reverse for every ten forward. The words from the March 27 *Utmost* reading carried meaning I couldn't have predicted at that time. But they lodged themselves in a dusty, rarely seen region of my heart.

For a decade after I copied those words on the inside cover of my Bible, I sought sanctification at every turn. If it was difficult, I did it. If it took sacrifice, it must be like Christ. If it made me a martyr, so be it. I was like an ascetic monk, flagellating my hands and feet and heart and bank account—the harder it hurt, the more I knew I was becoming like Christ in His sufferings. I believed He had marked out the path to Calvary's hill, and I was to follow in His every step, bearing my own cross, wearing the thorns, and accepting the beatings—even the ones I administered to myself. *This is how we gain insight*, I thought. If it doesn't hurt, it isn't real—and I wanted it to be real.

There is a passage from Margery Williams's story *The Velveteen Rabbit* that I had also written in my Bible:

"Real isn't how you are made," said the Skin Horse. "It's a thing that happens to you. When a child loves you for a long, long time, not just to play with, but REALLY loves you, then you become Real."

"Does it hurt?" asked the Rabbit.

"Sometimes," said the Skin Horse, for he was always truthful. "When you are Real you don't mind being hurt."

"Does it happen all at once, like being wound up," he asked, "or bit by bit?"

"It doesn't happen all at once," said the Skin Horse. "You become. It takes a long time. That's why it doesn't happen often to people who break easily, or have sharp edges, or who have to be carefully kept. Generally, by the time you are Real, most of your hair has been loved off, and your eyes drop out and you get loose in the joints and very shabby. But these things don't matter at all, because once you are Real you can't be ugly, except to people who don't understand."

I wanted my faith to be *real*. I knew it would be ugly, I knew it would take a long time, and I knew it would mean all my brokenness and sharp edges and fragility would need to become extinct. I needed to be perfect, I decided—only when my sanctification was complete would my faith become real.

A decade later, though, my faith felt less real than ever before—and so did God. I looked back over the chaos and pain of my life and felt God could not be real. Even if He was real, He could not be good, and even if He was good, He was not good to me, and therefore I could not serve a God who was good, but not to me. I closed my Bible, turned away from the truth of Scripture, nursed my misguided understanding of the gospel, and resented God deeply for years.

In many ways, the wandering that took place over the next season of my life was necessary. It was the "bit by bit" the Velveteen Rabbit had inquired about. I asked questions, I listened to stories of others who didn't believe in God, I searched out inconsistencies in Scripture. I pounced on any version of God that seemed at odds with another version as proof that He wasn't real or wasn't good. I became an expert at resenting the God I didn't think existed.

My old leather-bound Bible, used hard for a decade, was falling apart. An atheist friend noticed it and bought me a new one—a cheaper model this time, but the same words of life inside. I wrote nothing on the inside covers. I neglected it. It gathered dust much like the figurative dust settling over that Oswald Chambers quote somewhere in my heart.

This process of sanctification seemed to me only a way to grow more and more disillusioned with faith, God, the Bible, and other Christians. The more you grew, the more you realized how broken the world was—and how broken you were. Instead of leading to perfection, I learned, life in this world only made you more aware of how imperfect you were.

This insight, small though it was, became the seed that led me straight to grace. Surprised, I realized I had it all backward. I *was* broken. This world *was* broken. It was all so hopelessly broken there was no cure. No cure, that is, but One. Christ had walked the path to Calvary *so I didn't have to.* Christ had become my perfection because *I could never be perfect.* Christ had borne the penalty *I deserved.* Christ had gone up higher—and dropped down lower—so I could *grow in grace.*

So, one autumn morning, I scrawled those words of Oswald Chambers on the inside of my new Bible, where they still are, faded and smudged: "Growth in grace is measured not by the fact that you have not gone back, but that you have an insight into where you are spiritually; you have heard God say 'Come up higher,' not to you personally, but to the insight of your character."

In all my attempts to grow in the Christian life, to collect insight, and to improve in character, I had missed what Oswald Chambers was really saying. The grace he referred to was not my *own* poise or perfection, but what the cross offers to the children of God. My unattainable goal of growing—always moving forward and and higher—was leveled before the cross . . . the beautiful, sustaining, satisfying culmination of Christ on the cross. He is the one who says to me as I take ever failing, ever falling, ever faltering steps forward, "Come to me, you laborer, I will give you *rest*."

Christian, your growth in grace cannot be measured at all by means of your own making. Your scale is not accurate and your arms cannot spread wide enough. Your growth in grace is measured by God, your Father, beckoning you toward himself, showing His wide, deep, and extravagant love for you. His Spirit bears witness with the insight of your character, whispering words of grace, love, truth, and beauty. His Son has made a way to the cross by the way of the cross so that you do not have to bear the cross on your own.

This, my friends, is what "growth in grace" means for the child of God: seeing and savoring the great work of grace on our behalf. There is no game to be played, no going forward or going back—only greater insight into who your King is, and who you are because of that.

 Lore Ferguson Wilbert is a writer living in the Dallas area. She regularly writes for *Christianity Today* and She Reads Truth, and has written for The Gospel Coalition, Lifeway Leaders, and more. She writes at sayable.net and tweets @lorewilbert. She and her husband, Nate, have a dog, Harper, named after their favorite author, Harper Lee.

FAZALE RANA

*To be brought into the zone of the call
of God is to be profoundly altered.*
JANUARY 16, "THE VOICE OF THE NATURE OF GOD"

"Should I quit graduate school and pursue ministry?" It was nearly thirty years ago that I asked myself that question one evening, sitting at my lab bench in the chemistry department of Ohio University. I was a graduate student studying biochemistry. Only recently had I become a Christian, and I wondered how I could ever serve God as a scientist.

At the time, my wife, Amy, and I were attending Central Avenue United Methodist Church in Athens, Ohio. The college students I met there were singularly focused on preparing themselves for vocational ministry. They served as an example and an inspiration to me, yet I couldn't bring myself to follow suit. Maybe it was a lack of courage. Maybe a lack of commitment. Maybe it was because biochemistry came naturally to me. I was good at it, and studying the cell's molecular systems brought me joy.

My studies in biochemistry played a role in bringing me to faith in Christ. Though an agnostic when I started my graduate education, I became convinced that a Creator must be responsible for the origin of life—because I saw elegant, sophisticated, and ingenious designs in the cell's chemical systems. Amy, then my fiancée, had just rededicated her life to Christ and began to share her rediscovered faith with me. A pastor's challenge to read Scripture brought me face-to-face with my sin as I worked through the Sermon on the Mount. It also led to an encounter with Christ and His saving grace.

Though science played a key role in my conversion to Christianity, I had no vision for how I could use my knowledge and experience in science to serve the Lord. I was young in the faith, and I knew no one who could mentor me in this area. I felt like an odd duck: a Christian who was a scientist.

I decided to stay in graduate school. In fact, I earned my doctoral degree, completed two postdoctoral fellowships, and took a position in research and development at a Fortune 500 company. I also grew in my faith. At that time, one of the books that helped to deepen my relationship with God was Oswald Chambers's *My Utmost for His Highest*.

Amy's Aunt Mary Ellen gave me my first copy of the devotional shortly after I began my professional career. At that time I had no idea who Oswald Chambers was. Yet his book soon became a prized possession. I read it nearly every day, when I had a few minutes, keeping it on my office desk. Though each article was only a few paragraphs in length, the impact of Chambers's daily devotionals has been lasting, inspiring me to grow deeper in my intimacy with God and to live a life of holy dedication to Him.

The January 16 entry—"The Voice of the Nature of God"—was particularly challenging. Every time I read that entry, it took me back to the evening I sat at my lab bench mulling over the direction my life should take. In this piece, Chambers explores the idea of God's call on our lives and the way we should respond to it. Chambers points out that we can only recognize God's call if we have within us the same nature as "the One Who calls." He exhorts the reader to become like Isaiah, "so attuned to God" that His call penetrates our being.

The devotionals in *My Utmost for His Highest* are not "feel good" reads, by any means. In fact, they can be profoundly incisive, cutting to the core of the reader's soul. The January 16 entry did that very thing to me.

Having decided to stay in graduate school and pursue a career in science, I wondered if I was out of tune with God, so much so that I couldn't hear His voice. Or worse, had I clearly heard His call but refused to respond to it? Chambers had cautioned against dwelling on my own qualities and traits, thinking about what I was suited for instead of focusing on God's nature. Was that what I was doing?

Chambers also pointed out, as the updated edition of *My Utmost* says, "God providentially weaves the threads of His call through our lives, and only we can distinguish them." In my earliest days of faith, these words had little impact on me. But that's not surprising—I was still a young man. Intellectually, I could understand the idea of God's providence, but I couldn't grasp its deeper meaning. I hadn't experienced enough of life to be cognizant of the ways God was ordering my steps. Over the years, I've learned that it can be difficult to recognize God's providential workings when you are in the midst of an experience—it is only when you reflect on past events that God's guiding hand becomes evident.

Indeed, God was providentially weaving the threads of His call through my life. Thanks to my wife, I became obsessed with the interplay between science and faith. Amy was teaching biology at a local community college and, when she led the class through a section on evolution, she had her students write a paper on the creation-evolution controversy.

As resources for her students, Amy bought a number of books on the topic from a nearby Christian bookstore. After the class ended, she brought the books home. I picked up a few of them to read and was suddenly hooked. I read everything I could find on science-faith issues and the question of origins, regardless of the perspective.

Around this time, my father died. At his passing, he and I were estranged. My father was a Muslim, born in India, who came to the US in the 1950s. My mother was a non-practicing Catholic. She and my father agreed to disagree when it came to religion; as a result, my brother and I did not receive any sort of religious training, though my greatest exposure to any religion was to Islam. When I converted to Christianity, my father was furious and, in effect, disowned me.

Try as I might, I was unable to convince my father of the truth of Christianity, let alone reach him with the gospel. I was unaware of Christian apologetics as I helplessly watched my father die as a Muslim. Up to that point, evangelism hadn't been important to me, but my father's death forced me to see how vital it was to effectively explain, defend, and share my faith.

Shortly after his death, I prayed about my deep desire to be used by God to share the gospel. I didn't want to see anyone else die apart from the love of Christ. I distinctly remember telling God, "I'm not sure how you can use me—I know I'm only a scientist—but please use me to reach people with the gospel." Perhaps I really was attuned to God all along.

Soon I came to appreciate how powerful an ally science could be in defending and sharing the gospel. I remember seeing a book by Hugh Ross entitled *The Creator and the Cosmos*. In this work, Ross demonstrates how the latest advances in astronomy demonstrate God's existence and the reliability of the Scriptures. Then I became part of the team of volunteers who worked for Reasons to Believe, the ministry Ross cofounded with his wife, Kathy.

I learned that Hugh Ross wanted to build a team of scientists to work alongside him—men and women who were capable and willing to use science to build a bridge to the gospel. Amy and I had already had several conversations about my desire to focus full-time on science, apologetics, and evangelism. I imagined that I would do that in my retirement, but to my surprise, Amy encouraged me to contact Ross to let him know of my interest.

Inspired by this particular entry in *My Utmost*, I prayed Isaiah's response when God asked him, "Who should I send?" *Here I am, send me*. And God did. Since the summer of 1999, I have been on staff with Reasons to Believe, working as a scientist in ministry.

In retrospect, I see it would have been a mistake to quit graduate school and go into ministry. I could not have responded to God's call until God had fully intertwined His call through the events of my life.

I'm grateful for Biddy Chambers's diligence in faithfully recording her husband's teaching and publishing it after his death. Chambers's incisive words—which I have read on January 16 for a number of years now—prepared me to hear God's call and be forever changed.

Biochemist Fazale Rana is vice president of research and apologetics at Reasons to Believe, an organization dedicated to integrating scientific fact and biblical faith. His books include *The Cell's Design*, *Creating Life in the Lab*, and *Dinosaur Blood and the Age of the Earth*.

NATHANIEL LEE HANSEN

Your god may be your little Christian habit,
the habit of prayer at stated times, or the habit of
Bible reading. Watch how your Father will upset those
times if you begin to worship your habit instead of
what the habit symbolizes—"I can't do that just now,
I am praying; it is my hour with God."
No, it is your hour with your habit.
MAY 12, "MAKE A HABIT OF HAVING NO HABITS"

My Utmost for His Highest entered my life during the summer of 1998. I was working as a Bible-camp counselor in central Minnesota, the camp set beside a lake formed by a retreating glacier. Just as the landscape had undergone drastic alterations during the last ice age, I was undergoing a time of intense and difficult change—really a "renewing" and "remaking"—following the end of a two-year romantic relationship. Not knowing anyone at the camp other than the director who had interviewed me in the spring, I viewed the job as an opportunity to be refreshed and "reinvent myself."

During staff training—the two-week period before kids arrived—some other counselors referred to Chambers's book during a discussion of their "quiet time" practices. Shortly thereafter, at the local Christian bookstore, I bought a paperback copy for myself. I began reading it daily, the book becoming a part of the rhythm of my days.

I recall the way Chambers's words inspired me, encouraged me to pursue God more passionately, more deeply. I was already in an environment saturated with the religious: morning chapel, daily Bible study with my campers, evening campfire worship on the beach. However, I had never read anything that called me to such a high view of Jesus, of loving Him above all else. The book challenged me as no other book besides the Bible had until that point.

I lay on my sleeping bag in the cabin during the daily hour that counselors had "off," my charge of elementary-aged boys playing a game of capture the flag with the non-counselor staff. A small fan blew dusty cabin air on me as I stretched out, refreshed by my shower. I read a chapter or two from my study Bible, and after that, I read from Chambers. While I finished the remainder of my work day, I chewed on the words I had read. To say that Chambers's words entered my life at a critical time would be an understatement.

Since that summer, I've read through the entire book at least three more times, one time to my wife each night as part of our daily devotions. The last time I read through it, I underlined what I considered to be important statements—and *every* page has something underlined. It shows its wear through its condition: the spine is wrinkled like old skin.

I believe strongly in the value of spiritual disciplines, and throughout my years as a follower of Christ, I have practiced several in addition to time with *My Utmost*. Scripture reading and daily prayer have formed the core of my spiritual activities, besides the time devoted to corporate worship and small-group fellowship.

With Scripture reading, I have completed a few read-the-

Bible-in-one-year plans, and I've read the testaments at least a few times as well. I've focused on specific books, studying them intensely, using a variety of commentaries. I've incorporated plans that feature morning readings and evening readings.

With prayer, just as with Scripture reading, I've practiced various approaches. Perhaps the most common is the top-ten list of prayers that I prayed regularly. Some lasted a day or two; some lasted weeks and months. When God answered a prayer, I removed it from the list and added another petition. I've situated my prayer time at the end of the day; other times, I've placed it early in the morning. During one season, I rose at 5 a.m., and sat in the living room, Bible in my lap, notebook of prayers beside me, praying through each item individually. In short, I've marked many notebook pages over the years.

But for all of the good of the spiritual disciplines, there's a downside as well, and Oswald Chambers was aware of it. In the May 12 reading, "Make a Habit of Having No Habits," he reminds us that spiritual disciplines should be a means *to* God; they should not be a "stand-in" *for* God. I don't believe that Chambers was speaking explicitly against us forming practices, disciplines, or habits, but he was concerned that we avoid the trap of idolatry.

And that was a struggle I faced, feeling frustration when I would fall behind, forget, or not "complete" a particular spiritual discipline for the day. In my rigidity, I felt like I was a spiritual failure.

Ever since I was a young child, I have valued and desired control. I feel safest and most comfortable directing as much as I can about and in my circumstances; it's even better when I have a detailed plan written down somewhere. For me, control and planning live in the same house with me, kind of like a brother and sister. Growing up as I did with no biological siblings, my regular solitude likely contributed to this yearning for control. (I remember myself as a sixth grader, crafting a full day's schedule including the television shows I would watch, the different classes I would take, and, ultimately, all that I would do between rising and sleeping. The schedule, printed in blue ink on white paper, was push-pinned to my bedroom bulletin board. My parents were likely awed, but not surprised.)

My desire for control and my careful planning have served me well in my pursuits. They have successfully propelled me through a master's program and later doctoral studies. They have helped me as a writer, facilitating the drafting and revising of hundreds of poems, short stories, essays, reviews, and blog posts. As a university professor for the last six years, I would be less successful were it not for the control and planning that aid me in preparing, organizing, and teaching my courses.

But in the spiritual realm, when my discipline slipped, I would feel as though I was less than spiritual, that I was letting God down, that I was not getting "close to Him." I measured my spiritual well-being by my completion of practices, by acts of my will and body.

All too often in our faith journey, we can succumb to this temptation—to make spiritual practices and disciplines into our functional deity. But if the primary goal of spiritual disciplines is communion with God, then even these supposedly "good" practices can obstruct us. When I direct more energy toward the practices *themselves*, and less on the *end* of the practices, I am missing the point entirely. And if I continually focus my energy on those practices, I face another danger: that I am most concerned about maintaining control of my spiritual life. (The Lord knows how much I value control and planning.)

Looking back over my years of engaging in various spiritual disciplines, I have to admit, ashamedly, that most often my mindset was primarily to "get it done," to check something off my list for the day. I rarely, if ever, stopped to listen to what God might be saying; rarely, if ever, did I stop to be still. I was often treating the discipline, the activity, as *an end in itself*, and just another item on the full to-do list.

That's why Oswald Chambers warns us that if our attitudes toward disciplines and practices are misaligned, God "will upset those times." I am inclined to believe that my slow but gradual dissatisfaction with such rigid approaches was God's way of gaining my attention. There was never an audible voice—but reflecting now, it is clear to me that I was not open to God. So in recent years, I've moved away from such structured disciplines. Instead I find myself praying more randomly, more spontaneously, being led in the moment to uplift a request, a confession, a praise.

Perhaps that is what I take most from this text and from the totality of *My Utmost for His Highest*—wherever I am, whatever the time, I am to be attentive and open to God.

Nathaniel Lee Hansen is a poet and fiction writer who serves as an associate professor of English and Creative Writing at the University of Mary Hardin-Baylor in Belton, Texas. He edits *Windhover: A Journal of Christian Literature* and directs the annual Windhover Writers' Festival. His greatest joys are his wife, son, and daughter. He blogs at plainswriter.com.

MACY HALFORD

There is a darkness which comes
from excess of light.
JANUARY 19, "VISION AND DARKNESS"

I began reading *My Utmost for His Highest* the summer I was fifteen. From the start, I read it in a very particular way: I'd climb beneath the covers in the bedroom I shared with my sister, flashlight in hand, or else I'd shut myself in the closet, lingering long after the entry was done, letting the complexities of the message untie themselves in the dark.

At first, I read this way so as not to disturb my sister, but later I did it even when I was alone—Oswald was someone who seemed to *want* to be read in secret, for he had strange, secret things to tell, and he understood the importance of hiding to the spiritual life. "Shut the door and talk to God in secret," he said, speaking on Matthew 6:6. "It is impossible to conduct your life as a disciple without definite times of secret prayer" (September 16). *Utmost* was the first book I used as an opening act to my daily times of secret prayer, and it taught me how to do it well: in the quiet, in the dark, my mind illuminated by a single purpose.

That was in Texas in the 1990s, a decade which seemed

loud at the time but which I've come to think of as belonging to the *Blissful Before*—as in "Before the Fall," "Before the Flood," or, in my case, "Before New York" and "Before the Internet."

In the winter of 2004, shortly after I'd begun working as a blogger for a magazine with offices in Times Square, I moved with my roommates to an apartment one block south of Ground Zero. Right then, lots of young people were moving there, drawn by the relatively cheap rents that can sometimes be had in disaster zones—even disaster zones in lower Manhattan. My second week in the new place, I dialed 311, the number New Yorkers call to complain about anything and everything going on in the city. (It's a busy line.) I explained that there were trucks and diggers and cranes and cement mixers passing by my building twenty-four hours a day, every day. It was so loud, I said, that my roommates and I had to shout to hear each other over dinner. It was so loud that we hadn't slept in days. It was so loud that we couldn't get any work done. I had to blog, I told the 311 guy. For the *Internet*. Did he understand what that meant?

"*It's Ground Freakin' Zero,*" the guy replied. "Buy some earplugs."

I bought some earplugs.

As the months passed, I gradually became accustomed to my new home. I'd work at the window in my bedroom, looking out on a tableau that was both apocalyptic and reassuring—like something Richard Scarry might have drawn if he were channeling Hieronymus Bosch. While the cranes and diggers and hard-hatted workers maneuvered their way cheerfully around the pit, soldiers—their machine guns pointed studiously at the ground—patrolled the barbed-wire barrier, keeping watch over a constant stream of selfie-snapping tourists.

My eyes would drift from this weird new world to the one on my screen, which felt somehow even weirder and newer, this Internetland I was obliged to travel into constantly, searching for content, monitoring content, creating content. Now, as often as not, it was here that I read Oswald Chambers, clicking absent-mindedly at the bookmark I'd set for the daily reading of *Utmost*.

What's amazing to me, looking back on those days, is that I thought that life would inevitably return to a quieter state. Once the pit was filled in or I'd moved to a different neighborhood or I'd graduated from blogging to "real" writing, things—by which I primarily meant my ability to concentrate—would slip back to the way they'd been. Noise and distraction and chaos of this magnitude were not normal or natural, I thought, and couldn't possibly endure for long.

Oswald knew that life didn't work this way. During his own lifetime, friends called him "the Apostle of the Haphazard" because he'd preached that tragedy was the basis of things, and that days of perplexity were never far from days of peace. In *Utmost*, the idea helped to form one of his grand themes.

Our faith, he argued, must be in God himself, not in a rosy idea of God. Who was God? He was a God who worked in haphazard ways, a God who was not synonymous with His blessings, and whose "permissive will" defied common sense and our own expectations. And Oswald did not think that this kind of faith—childlike and warriorlike at once, rising to all occasions, accepting and embracing all possibilities, even the most horrific—came easily. Faith was a journey, a "discipline," to be honed over time like a craft. He compared life to an ocean in a tempest, full of crashing waves that struck fear in the ordinary swimmer, but which gave the seasoned surfer "the super joy of going clean through it" (March 7).

In 2004, I was just an ordinary swimmer, struggling to keep my head above water, convinced that the tempest around me would soon die down. But long after I'd moved and stopped blogging, long after the pit had been filled in and 9/11 had drifted far into memory, the noise and confusion continued.

Slowly, I began to understand that the new reality, which seemed so unreal, was here to stay. I didn't work for the Internet anymore, yet it remained a dominating, distracting presence in my life. The pit outside my own window might have been filled in, but there was always fresh terror *some-where*—and, thanks to the Internet, I was always, intimately, aware of it. The Internet was a world constantly on high alert, and it demanded constant vigilance.

Everyone I knew *was* vigilant, faithfully following the news, reading e-mail, watching TV shows, chatting with friends, checking up on acquaintances, broadcasting opinions. I didn't think that these things were wrong, in and of themselves. They were versions of things humans had always done, and they were in a sense unavoidable: one couldn't switch off the Internet without cutting oneself off from others. But there seemed to be a link between this new mode of life—the constant, kinetic, anxious gathering and dispersing of information—and an increasingly anxious atmosphere. Steeped in an endless stream of violent news and outraged commentary, even my most easygoing friends were becoming outraged and inflexible. Constantly updated on the minutiae of other people's lives, they were becoming less content with their own.

One January evening, I picked up *My Utmost* and read this line: "There is a darkness which comes from excess of light." It was a perfect description of information overload, and it seemed to literally describe the Internet—the illuminated screen that darkened everything beyond its tiny frame. I'd read the line before, but this time I was surprised by what came next. (No matter how many times I read *Utmost*, it could always manage to surprise me.)

Oswald spoke of the darkness not as something to fear, but as something to appreciate for its own special qualities. Darkness, he said, was a place not for doing but for waiting and listening. If we lacked clarity and direction, if we were paralyzed, unable to turn the maelstrom of our thoughts into action, we were to be still and to wait on God. He would speak, eventually. Darkness was God's, Oswald said, an instrument He used to guide us beyond our usual sources of light to the single *true* source, the light which contained and commanded the darkness. When we felt ourselves trapped in darkness, that was God holding us "in the shadow of His hand."

It is in these moments, when God forcibly turns our faces toward Him, that everything else begins to fade into its proper place. It is so easy for us to lapse into thinking that our circumstances are "too much for God" (July 4), that in their weirdness and newness they are distant from Him. We treat "the things that happen as if they were engineered by men" (December 18), instead of perceiving His hand behind all.

The message struck me powerfully. There was perhaps nothing that seemed as man-made to me as the Internet, and over the years I'd often followed man-made advice about dealing with it. I'd "unplugged," limited myself to reading the news just once a day, called people on the phone instead of e-mailing. Oswald's message, advising something far beyond simple avoidance or temperance, made me begin to see God in places I'd never thought to look: in fiberglass tubes that carried tiny pulses of light across the ocean floor; in lines of code that smashed up images and put them back together again; in gangs of trolls that roamed online chat rooms, seeking prey; in videos of bomb explosions on Twitter; in my own eyesight, growing weaker with every passing year spent before the screen. In all these places and more, I began to see the hand of God . . . and to accept the feelings they inspired.

These are still feelings of bafflement, and the future—when I attempt to gaze into it—still appears darker to me than the past. But I've begun to feel myself progressing from ordinary swimmer to seasoned surfer. The sky above is often mottled and gray; the waves are high. Many times, they knock me from my board. Before, I would have struggled to the surface, gasping for air, filled with panic. Now, I've learned to stay under, in the dark and the confusion, to hold my breath and to wait.

Macy Halford was born and grew up in Dallas, Texas. She graduated from Barnard College and later worked at *The New Yorker*, where she edited and wrote the online book review. Knopf released her book, *My Utmost: A Devotional Memoir*, in February 2017. She now lives in Paris.

PATRICIA RAYBON

Our heavenly Father knows the circumstances
we are in, and if we keep concentrated
on Him we will grow spiritually as the lilies.
MAY 18, "CAREFUL UNREASONABLENESS"

He's the gangly young fisherman in a grainy old photo (*see frontispiece*)—standing on a rock, wearing country clothes, looking content to cast a fly rod over a shallow Yorkshire stream, waiting for a bite. Enjoying the wait.

This is Oswald Chambers, man of nature—and as a Colorado-grown believer, I delighted in discovering this outdoor image of the theological man. It's a strong contrast to my first introduction to Chambers. Then, I was struggling in work and life, wrestling to blaze a trail as a "successful" black author. On a bookshelf, however, I found *My Utmost for His Highest*—coaxing me to stop fighting to be "more."

Instead, be broken. "Broken bread and poured-out wine" before God—the phrase appears ten times in *Utmost*. This is classic Chambers, urging disciples to abandon our all to gain the lowly but sufficient Christ. So I plunged, falling heart-first into Chambers's deep well of wise, clarifying, terrifying humility. I couldn't get enough. As with those deer panting

63

for water brooks (Psalm 42:1), I lapped up the evangelist's wisdom to surrender—to die in Christ in order to live free.

God knows I had tried. I am a Coloradan, but I'm also black, indeed. Life has poured me out flat, pinning me to the ground more than a few times with racial hurt, which stings badly. Now here was Chambers telling me to bring that pain to Jesus, to lay myself down at His feet to be broken up even more.

It seemed biblical and right, but so hard. Thus, I kept trying. Trying to give all, and failing. Trying to love more, and refusing. Trying to match my life to Chambers's words and ways, and still falling short.

Then, years later, after still too many seasons of self-striving, I finally lay down my arms at the Cross—only to meet the simple and surrendered Chambers there, too.

Who was he? A saint who loved his sovereign Lord, and taught His strong Word without compromise. Chambers also knew, however, that God can be found not just in healing words or life struggle, but in the soft grace of a warm day. In a starry night. On an afternoon of fishing. Beside a Yorkshire Dales stream on a clear morning. Chambers's description for such simple abandon? "Careful unreasonableness."

There, in such places and moments, the best thing to do is simply thank God, as friends recalled him saying, for "the leagues of pure air."

So I take one long, deep breath.

It's a clear, fresh day. Outside, I hear my husband raking away dead winter grass and vines from our yard while birds sing overhead. Sunshine warms the April air.

It's an oddly proper Chambers moment—no hurry in it, even as the birdsong and the gardening sounds and the day's work declare together that God is in His universe and in Him, all can be right with our often sorrowful, divided world.

Chambers, considering the birds, taught, "Song birds are taught to sing in the dark and we are put into the shadow of God's hand until we learn to hear him" (February 14).

Only a man who has listened to God's creation—even in the midst of war, loss, spiritual struggle and other upheaval— can speak with such confidence. Drawn by his clear-eyed trust, I turn to one of Chambers's "outdoor" reflections, one I'd somehow missed before. My well-worn copy of *My Utmost* is marked at the places of my own desperation and Chambers's toughest rigor: "If you have the whine in you, kick it out ruthlessly" (April 14).

I have eaten up this strident Chambers. The tougher the teaching, the better.

A few pages ahead, however, in a lesson with nary a single underlined word, there is Chambers reflecting about lilies. Consider, he says, how they grow: they neither toil nor spin—"they simply *are*!"

I float on this reminder, appreciating the relaxed nature of the fresh-air Chambers: "Think of the sea, the air, the sun, the stars, and the moon," he says. "All of these simply *are*— yet what a ministry and service they render on our behalf" (updated edition).

It's his call to cease striving and, as Chambers says, simply *be* in Christ.

This is surrender, of course, and I sink into it with relief. As an African-American of a certain attitude and age, surrender in Christ is like a salve.

Chambers goes on: "The people who influence us the most are not those who detain us with their continual talk, but those who live their lives like the stars in the sky and 'the lilies of the field'—simply and unaffectedly. Those are the lives that mold and shape us" (updated edition).

As a lifetime resident of Colorado, where the birds of the

air, the flowers of the field and the stars of the sky have provided such a gracious and godly blessing, I rush to embrace this Chambers of the open air.

What do I find? God's light.

Stopping to read the entire devotional again, I finally see what I'd missed before. This isn't a celebration *of* nature—it's a borrowing *from* nature, showing how birds and trees, flora and fauna, sun and stars, moon and sky "simply are" because they're not trying to be more.

This hits home hard. In my life as an African-American—finding myself judged, ridiculed, second-guessed, suspected, and rejected in moments throughout my life—I have worked overtime to counteract by being more.

Once, after getting a teaching position at a large university, I came *this close* to ruining my health, laboring around the clock, determined to prove myself worthy of employment at such an "important" institution.

For me, it was a "race issue." For countless others, however, this same struggle to "make it" or to "be enough" in the world's eyes becomes a lifetime of strain and effort.

Instead, says Chambers, stop the striving. Simply focus on the Lord. Nothing more is asked. That's the lesson of Matthew 6:26—"Look at the birds of the air."

Of course those birds, as Jesus understood, only *appear* carefree and unworried. Jesus knew (as did the nature-loving Chambers) that birds are among the most vulnerable creatures on Earth. Almost all are potential prey for some hungry predator. Meantime, modern dangers—window panes, high tension lines, cars, wind turbines, pesticides, oil spills—are constant threats.

Consider the birds?

They neither sow nor reap or store away in barns, and yet? "Your heavenly Father feeds them."

Watching birds at a state park near our house, my husband and I marvel, indeed, at their trust. A gorgeous black-billed magpie glides from tree to cattail stand to fence post to shrub, landing with a final swooping twirl that resembles a dance of outright joy. *I am alive and loved by my Creator.* Apparently trusting that this is enough, the bird takes off again and soars—the sight a "ministration" to our souls, Chambers says.

So consider the birds, says Christ. "Are you not much more valuable than they?"

Too often, Chambers says, "we mar God's designed influence through us by our self-conscious effort to be consistent and useful. [But] Jesus says that there is only one way to develop spiritually, and that is by concentration on God."

Turn attention from ourselves, focusing on God and His Creation, "and out of you will flow rivers of living water."

Looking at this photo of Chambers—so relaxed, so content, so available just to fish in a stream made by the God he knew and trusted—we can be astonished at what the man accomplished. Without even trying, he became one of the most beloved devotional teachers of the entire world. Without trying.

He longed for people to know the God of the Bible, as taught in the Holy Word. But to be the most published devotional writer of all time? Chambers never sought it.

Here's the nugget, from the updated edition of *My Utmost*: "If you want to be of use to God, maintain the proper relationship with Jesus Christ by staying focused on Him, and He will make use of you every minute you live—yet you will be unaware, on the conscious level of your life, that you are being used of Him."

To be sure, if we knew that God *was* using us in some extraordinary way, we would be insufferable with conceit.

Better to go fishing.

When I was a kid, my black Daddy did that. Deep in the Colorado mountains, far from the racial struggle of his desk job in the city, he took his tackle box and fly rod to a trickling stream. And his family traipsed along.

Watching him in his faded fishing gear and old cowboy hat, I perhaps never felt more safe and right. On those days, we weren't keeping up with the Joneses, navigating church politics, aiming for excellence in life, fighting racism, battling self-doubt, or even seeking to serve the lost.

Instead, we sought God. And what a wonder—He was waiting. Enjoying even us. As Chambers taught, He still is.

Patricia Raybon's personal essays on family and faith have been published in the *New York Times Magazine*, *Newsweek*, *USA Today*, *USA Weekend*, *Country Living Magazine*, *Chicago Tribune*, *The Denver Post*, *Guideposts*, *In Touch Magazine* (In Touch Ministries), *Christianity Today*, and popular blogs including *Her.Meneutics* and the *Washington Post's Acts of Faith*, as well as airing on National Public Radio. She's the award-winning author of five books.

DEREK MOUNT

When someone thinks that to develop a holy life
he must always be alone with God,
he is no longer of any use to others.
FEBRUARY 24, "THE DELIGHT OF SACRIFICE"
(UPDATED EDITION)

In a cloud of black exhaust, the disheveled Nissan Altima clunked its way in front of me at the Atlanta airport pickup line. When the passenger door flopped open, I peeled my guitar case off my sweaty back and tossed it on top of a crinkled bag of Peanut Butter Ritz Bits lying in the back seat. Hopping into the front, I extended my hand, only to be greeted by the most genuine hug a touring musician could ever dream of receiving. Then my warm, witty friend Isaac shifted his $650 car into gear, and we puttered toward the interstate.

On the highway, he shouted, trying to make his voice audible above the air pummeling us through the open windows. "You ready to see the Thunderdome?" Excitement animated his smiling face, his red beard dancing as he regaled me with stories of his housemates. After a couple of hilarious tales, I concluded that the "Thunderdome" (I choose to capitalize it) was the name he had given to his residence, a rental house filled to the brim with ambitious filmmakers. I was impressed by the affection he felt toward his home and, more importantly, his peers.

I entered the house fully expecting to discover an unkempt bachelor pad—after all, I was contributing to the artist stereotype by crashing on Isaac's couch (or floor, depending on which was available) between tour dates. Inside, I was pleased to find a place unlike any other in which I'd previously shacked.

A cinnamon-roll scented candle burned on the kitchen table, the flame dancing to the beat of a Radiohead album playing in the top-floor bedroom. A white bedsheet dangled from the living room wall, taking a nap from the Mario Kart tournaments and short-film viewings repeatedly projected upon it. Creative energy pulsed throughout the house, as tapping keyboards and clicking mouse buttons polished passion projects.

One of the younger residents emerged from his room and brought me up to speed on the 'dome. The roommates worked together, he said, sharing everything—gigs, contacts, ideas, even meals. Most of them had moved to the city from small towns, and now they were creating and growing together under this one roof. The bustling brotherhood was alive, a profound, intentional collective. It was inspirational.

"I love it," I declared, sitting down to a bowl of goat's milk yogurt. "You've created a commune!"

Isaac, chewing an uncooked green bean, replied, "I prefer to think of it as more of a community."

The Thunderdome sprang to mind when I read the February 24 entry of *My Utmost for His Highest*. Oswald Chambers asserts that "when someone thinks that to develop a holy life he must always be alone with God, he is no longer of any use to others." Cooperation and service, the power and importance of community, are paramount themes in the message of Christ. Or, as Chambers puts it, "Once 'the love of God has been poured out in our hearts by the Holy Spirit,' we deliberately begin to identify ourselves with Christ's interests and purposes in others' lives (Romans 5:5)."

We recognize this concept in the book of Matthew, as Jesus declares, "Where two or three gather in my name, there am I with them" (Matthew 18:20). Similarly, through the creation story's emphasis on Eve, we perceive the message that we desperately need one another. "The LORD God said, 'It is not good for the man to be alone'" (Genesis 2:18). Furthermore, the letters of the apostle Paul are filled with "one another" commands—love one another (Romans 13:8), honor one another (Romans 12:10), accept one another (Romans 15:7), live in harmony with one another (Romans 12:16), encourage one another (2 Corinthians 13:11), be kind and compassionate to one another (Ephesians 4:32), serve one another, in love (Galatians 5:13).

The spirit of fellowship is essential to the human experience, enabling us to really understand what it means to be alive. Christ came in His full humanity to lead us into our full humanity—and without others, this could never be realized. Our deepest, most meaningful experiences in life would be impossible in isolation—falling in love, becoming a parent, hearing a story, sharing a meal.

"While we instinctively pursue our own intimacy with God, it is often through interaction with others that we find our most complete connection with the holy. In the absence of others, the message of Christ feels empty, and finding a sense of significance proves challenging.

That is why Oswald Chambers says, "When someone thinks that to develop a holy life he must always be alone with God, he is no longer of any use to others. That is like putting himself on a pedestal and isolating himself from the rest of society. Paul was a holy person, but wherever he went Jesus Christ was always allowed to help Himself to his life. Many of us are interested only in our own goals, and Jesus cannot help Himself to our lives. But if we are totally surrendered to Him, we have no goals of our own to serve."

Chambers references Paul's devotion to Christ, which made him willing "to be a 'doormat' without resenting it," and presents an invitation to all of us to participate in love as a lifestyle, rather than a task to check off a to-do list. As I reflect on my personal faith journey, I am grateful to have been able to participate in church events, mission trips, music tours, community improvement initiatives, and other special projects that have served as opportunities to extend grace outwardly. But it is the day in, day out authenticity of the Thunderdome that captures my imagination, this real-world example of Oswald Chambers's teaching on the others-centered life. The February 24 entry of *My Utmost for His Highest* is accompanied by the verse that Chambers often quoted in his ministry: "I will very gladly spend and be spent for your souls" (2 Corinthians 12:15 NKJV).

This is, according to Chambers, "one of the greatest tests of our relationship with Jesus Christ. The delight of sacrifice is that I lay down my life for my Friend, Jesus (see John 15:13). I don't throw my life away, but I willingly and deliberately lay it down for Him and His interests in other people."

The Thunderdome, which has now expanded to include the house next door, is a manifestation of a dream Isaac described to me years ago, and it takes seriously Chambers's summons to lay down one's life for the sake of Jesus. We observe this by reaching out to and serving others.

Every now and then, we see what life can be like when we step out of solitude and into community—we sharpen one another, we offer compassion, we foster diversity, we experience acceptance, we grow, we create, we share, we love. And the greatest of these is love.

Derek Mount is a guitarist, composer, songwriter, and producer. He has cowritten eight number one hits and fifteen top ten songs across various radio formats and released three albums under the moniker of his cinematic instrumental project, Brique a Braq. Derek's songs have been used in feature films, commercials, television programs, retail stores, sporting events, and corporate presentations. He spent eleven and a half years as lead guitarist for the electro-pop band Family Force 5 and has appeared as a special guest for several artists. When not on tour, Derek performs at local churches, teaches online guitar lessons, and works as a session player. He lives with his wife, Sarah, in Atlanta, Georgia.

MICHELLE ULE

Prayer is not a question of altering things externally,
but of working wonders in a man's disposition.
AUGUST 28, "WHAT'S THE GOOD OF PRAYER?"

Prayer is a major theme throughout *My Utmost for His Highest,* and Oswald Chambers's perspective is encapsulated in the October 17 reading: "Prayer does not fit us for the greater works; prayer *is* the greater work."

I first read *My Utmost* late in my spiritual walk—twenty-five years after I became a Christian. By that point, I thought I knew how to pray.

God used life and Oswald Chambers to show me otherwise.

As a child, I had learned to pray with the familiar words, "Our Father, who art in heaven." Early on, I thirsted for spiritual truth, and the idea that the Creator of the universe listened to my prayers both comforted and astonished me. As a teenager, I learned that God's willingness to hear my prayers was the result of Jesus's death on the cross.

Jesus's sacrifice meant I could tell Him anything about my life—especially the sins—and savor the forgiving peace that passes all understanding. What an exciting concept, this idea that God wanted to communicate with me! Then I learned that praying for others—intercessory prayer—served an important role in God's kingdom. Since all sorts of people appreciate prayer, I happily obliged them.

Given a choice, I preferred not to know too many details. I appreciated Oswald's admonition, "if you know too much, more than God has engineered for you to know, you cannot pray, the condition of the people is so crushing that you cannot get through to reality" (December 13).

I felt freer to pray, in accordance with the Holy Spirit's leading, when I didn't have specifics. Rather than a recitation of requests, my prayers became broader, an attempt to match a person's perceived need with biblical promises. Too often, however, I asked God to act the way I suggested based solely on my opinion.

In response, God took me on a journey. He wanted me to learn that the heart of all prayer takes us back to Him, deepening our relationship with Him. To help me understand, God used a *My Utmost* entry to save me from despair over the seeming failure of prayers I had whispered for years.

Long ago a friend asked me to pray for her daughter. This young woman had returned from her freshman year of college sullen and changed. My friend couldn't understand what had happened, and the girl deflected her questions.

I'd prayed for this family for years. I'd celebrated with my friend and her husband the Sunday they carried their long-desired baby to the baptismal font. I was the little girl's first babysitter. I'd watched her and her siblings grow up, through pictures in Christmas cards and through visits to their home.

My practice of prayer was to lift up requests the first couple of days after someone asked, but then to let those needs "float," awaiting promptings from the Holy Spirit. When God would bring a person or request to mind, I prayed.

At that time, our church's Sunday service featured a pause during corporate worship, a time for us to murmur our personal requests. My mind roamed the country, and I silently prayed for an ailing aunt in California, elderly acquaintances in Connecticut, stressed friends in Texas, and so on. I thought of my friend's daughter nearly every Sunday morning, usually praying for her around nine o'clock.

In talking to God, I mentioned the young woman's safety, her estrangement from her family, the environment she lived in, her studies, and whatever else made sense at the time. She came to mind regularly, for years.

One summer day, I picked up a book about some distressing activities taking place at American universities. Because I had a daughter preparing for college, I wanted to know more about the trends so I could better counsel my child in advance.

The author structured the book around interviews with college women who described their experiences and the reasons behind their choices. My stomach churned as I read about intelligent women debasing themselves for men's attention.

I shook my head over the actions and the women's justification for their behavior. The book disturbed me, but I pushed through it. I wanted to understand the thinking behind these behaviors, particularly to help the young women I served as a lay counselor.

The journalist masked the women's personal facts, using made-up names for each. But in one chapter I recognized the girl at once.

I reread the details, trying to find discrepancies to eliminate my suspicions, but it had to be her. I personally knew family incidents that were important elements in this young woman's life.

My friend's daughter, the girl I'd been praying for on Sunday mornings, had participated in soul-deadening activities at college, often *on* Sunday mornings. My brain flipped through memory after memory, recalling the love of this young woman's parents and their worries.

I clenched my fists and and my whole body shook. "What's the good of praying, then, if this is what happens?" I spat at God.

Over the years, I had not prayed as much for any person other than my own children. I could not comprehend how an intelligent woman, raised in a God-honoring home, could behave in such a way—or how futile my prayers had been if this was the result of them.

In disgust I spun away from God, down into a black hole of disappointment and grief.

Despite years of sharing everything with God—and countless glorious answers to my requests—I saw no point in continuing to pray if this woman's experience was the outcome.

My family noticed my distress, but I couldn't explain the situation without breaking a confidence. I didn't want to be consoled. I didn't want to pray—about anything, any more.

But praying without ceasing—talking to God continuously—had been part of my life for so long, it was hard to simply turn off the habit. Logic pushed in. Faith called out. Anguish cried no! This misery didn't want company.

One day, though, the Holy Spirit broke through, asking me why I would allow one foolish woman's choices to destroy my own relationship with God.

The Person who best understood my hurt and misery was waiting for me to bring my heart to Him. We'd gone through hard times before, and I knew He would listen. I missed Him, and I knew that only Jesus's sacrificial love could soothe my hurt.

In trepidation, on August 28 I picked up *My Utmost for His Highest* to start an awkward time with God. I nearly dropped the book when I read that day's title: "What's the Good of Prayer?"

Isn't that what I had demanded to know?

Here was Oswald Chambers's answer: "Prayer is the way the life of God is nourished. Our ordinary views of prayer are not found in the New Testament. We look upon prayer as a means of getting things for ourselves; the Bible idea of prayer is that we may get to know God Himself."

God often stabs my conscience when I read *My Utmost*.

I had prayed for this girl as an inoculation—hoping to save her and her family from pain and confusion. When I discovered the apparent results, I jettisoned God rather than refocus the prayers.

In refusing to pray, I had cut myself off from the God who loved *her* more than I did, from the God who could comfort *me* and help me process what a young woman had sought in place of His love.

Tears filled my eyes as I reasoned with God, asking for forgiveness and help. And He showed me that my prayers had had some good results. According to the book's account, I could see that I had prayed for the girl during some physically dangerous times. My prayers did not keep her from bad judgment, but may have protected her on several documented occasions.

The young woman is an adult now, and she long ago set aside her college behavior. She regrets the book interview. Her relationship with her family is sound and loving. God still is working on her heart, and my prayers for her continue.

So maybe there had been good in those prayers. But Oswald Chambers gave a definite answer to the question, "What's the good of prayer?" That August 28 entry explains, "It is not so true that 'prayer changes things' as that prayer changes *me*."

My expectation of the One who can and does answer my prayers has matured. Now I see myself as called to pray no matter how the outcome looks. I weep with Jesus, and I ask the Holy Spirit to intervene in ways that I cannot.

Now I pray for God's will and His glory, and for Jesus to be better known—by me and by the people for whom I pray. I ask for truth to be revealed to those who need to know. The circumstances may not change and the apparent answers may not be pretty, but my response is to turn them all over to God. No matter what happens—even if I don't understand—I will trust Him with the people He loves.

Thanks be to God.

Thanks for Oswald Chambers, who taught God's prayer lessons, and for Biddy Chambers, who compiled them into *My Utmost for His Highest*.

Amen.

Longtime prayer intercessor Michelle Ule is the author of *Mrs. Oswald Chambers*, a biography of Biddy Chambers. A Bible study leader for more than thirty years, Michelle lives with her family in Northern California. You can learn more about Michelle, and read her many blog posts about Oswald and Biddy Chambers, at michelleule.com.

AMY PETERSON

If you make usefulness the test,
then Jesus Christ was
the greatest failure that ever lived.
AUGUST 30, "AM I CONVINCED BY CHRIST?"

I wanted to ignore the cries. It was two a.m., after all, no time for any reasonable person to be getting out of bed. But my eight-week-old son, Owen, was not a reasonable person—not yet. He was simply unreasonable when it came to milk. And if I didn't get to him quickly, he'd wake his two-year-old sister, too. I pulled myself out of my soft bed and padded down the hallway to him.

As I rocked Owen in the dark room, my sleep-deprived mind wandered. What had I gotten myself into?

In the last year, I'd moved with my husband and daughter across the country to a tiny town in the middle of a corn-field—where I didn't know a soul. I'd given birth. I'd spent most days with these two tiny children in my house while my husband taught at a local university. I was doing good if I could just keep us all bathed and fed and somewhat rested. I rarely had the mental capacity to read a book, much less teach a class or lead a small group.

I thought of all the things I had been able to accomplish with my days *before* I became a mother. In college I had led Bible studies, won academic awards, backpacked through the Grand Canyon and Europe. In my twenties I'd gone to graduate school and spent two years as a missionary in Southeast Asia. There I'd introduced Jesus to people who had never even heard His name. I'd seen a church begin to form where no church had been before. I had taught classes in English and Bible to middle schoolers, high schoolers, and college students. I had made a difference. I had done big things for God.

Now I was reduced to diapers and pacifiers, dirty dishes and play dough. I spent hours pretending to be a jungle cat with the toddler and days bouncing the colicky baby. It wasn't that I didn't love my children or think taking care of them was important—it just didn't feel as valuable to the kingdom as the work I had once been able to do. I wanted to address the inequalities of the world, fight for justice, feed the hungry, provide jobs for the poor, tell people about the love of Jesus. I wanted to be useful to God.

This wasn't the first time I'd despaired because the work I was given to do seemed unimportant in the face of the world's great needs. I'd felt the same way even when I had been a missionary, teaching English in Cambodia. Those classes had seemed less important than the justice work other missionaries around me were doing.

I'd felt the same way in college. The Twin Towers fell early in my sophomore year, and as I watched the news, I wanted to drop out of school. What was the point in taking Business Math and French II when there was so much pain, so much need in the world?

I stayed in college, though, and Oswald Chambers was one who helped convince me to stay. In the August 30 entry of *My Utmost for His Highest*, Chambers reflects on the words of Jesus in Luke 10. Seventy-two of Jesus's followers had journeyed ahead of Him, spreading word of His kingdom, and they returned to Jesus rejoicing because of all they'd been able to do. Jesus warned them, "Do not rejoice in this, that the spirits are subject to you, but rather rejoice because your names are written in heaven" (Luke 10:20 NKJV). Here's how Chambers interprets Jesus's words:

> Jesus Christ says, in effect, Don't rejoice in successful service, but rejoice because you are rightly related to Me. The snare in Christian work is to rejoice in successful service, to rejoice in the fact that God has used you. You never can measure what God will do through you if you are rightly related to Jesus Christ. Keep your relationship right with him, then whatever circumstances you are in, and whoever you meet day by day, He is pouring rivers of living water through you, and it is of His mercy that He does not let you know it.

As I prayed about it that autumn, I determined to stay in college. I would focus on my relationship with Jesus and do the tasks that were set before me. I would try to do them well, hoping to be faithful in the "small things" so that God would entrust me with bigger things in the future (Luke 16:11).

But several years later, as a missionary in Cambodia, having finally done some of those "bigger things," I found myself thinking through Chambers's words again. God reminded me that I was not the best judge of what work was valuable. Rejoicing in my ability to be useful or "to do big things" for Him was dangerous—rather, I needed to rejoice in my relationship with God as His beloved child.

I began to see that my desire to be "useful to God" might actually be more about *me* than about God's kingdom. I wanted to be useful to God because I wanted to be important, valuable, lovable. But God had already loved me. He had called me beloved. If I were able to rest confidently in my identity as His child, I would no longer need to strive to be useful; I could trust that God was working through me as He wanted.

Having learned this lesson twice, you might think that by the time I reached motherhood—finding myself housebound and consumed with quotidian tasks—I would have been prepared. But, in fact, throughout my life I find myself constantly returning to this lesson. I have to remind myself again and again that God does not measure us by our "usefulness" to His kingdom.

Of course, this is not an excuse to let injustice go unchecked, or to turn a blind eye to the needs of our world. My desire to do "big things" for God is partly about my own pride, but partly an authentic—and, I think, Spirit-guided—response to the very real brokenness I see around me. It's not necessarily wrong to want to be useful to the kingdom. But I get into trouble when I try to measure my own service, or when I make usefulness the "ground of appeal," as Chambers says. "The lodestar of the saint is God Himself, not estimated usefulness." I get into trouble when I make my own work the focus, rather than my relationship with God.

We are never able to measure our own usefulness to the kingdom. We can't see our lives or our world from God's perspective. After all, Chambers says provocatively, "If we make usefulness the test, then Jesus Christ was the greatest failure that ever lived." From a limited human perspective, that's true: Jesus entered a world that was full of political corruption, social inequality, unfair taxation, illness, poverty, hunger—and when he left thirty-three years later, there were no visible changes in any of those areas. He died without changing the world.

Or at least that's how it looked.

Jesus lived a life of humility, sacrificing when He was asked to sacrifice, and remaining in fellowship with the Father. Isn't that what we're called to do, too? When we are delighting in God, we can be confident that He'll be "pouring rivers of living water" through us in whatever work we do (see John 7:38).

Our work is valuable not because we feel like we're doing important things, but because God imbues whatever we do—even diaper changing and playing pretend with pre-schoolers—with meaning and purpose. We are valuable not because of our service, but because God himself has loved us.

Amy Peterson lives with her husband and children on two acres of Indiana farmland and teaches and works with the Honors program at Taylor University. With a B.A. in English Literature from Texas A&M and an M.A. in Intercultural Studies from Wheaton College, Amy taught ESL for two years in Southeast Asia before returning stateside to teach in California, Arkansas, and Washington. She is a regular contributor to *Our Daily Bread* and *Off the Page*. She has written for *Books & Culture*, *Christianity Today*, *The Other Journal*, *Comment Magazine*, *The Cresset*, *The Living Church*, and *Art House America*, among other outlets. She is the author of *Dangerous Territory: My Misguided Quest to Save the World*.

GEORGE GRANT

Bethel is the symbol of communion with God;
Ai is the symbol of the world.
Abraham pitched his tent between the two.
JANUARY 6, "WORSHIP"

It was nearly half a century ago that I began to make my way through the classic book *My Utmost for His Highest*. It was the very first daily devotional I'd ever read, and it had an immediate, powerful, and enduring impact.

Very quickly, I found a host of Oswald Chambers's memorable phrases making their way from the pages of that little red hardcover into my daily conversation: "broken bread and poured-out wine" (numerous entries, including February 2), "prayer *is* the greater work" (October 17), "the strain of waiting" (February 22), "we are built for the valley" (October 1), "do what is not your duty" (July 14), "when you are in the dark, listen" (February 14), "unhasting and unresting" (January 6), and "humbling . . . to our religious conceit" (November 14). Day after day, I found Chambers's wisdom to be pungent and picturesque—enabling me to taste and see the profoundest truths of the gospel with a potent practicality. To this day, I still do.

As a result, the thought of choosing a single passage from *My Utmost* is an almost ludicrous notion—it is the whole book taken together, it is the entirety of the life and ministry of Oswald Chambers, it is the compounding and cumulative effect of the complete oeuvre that has so shaped my Christian life. Even so, there *is* one entry that particularly bolsters my faith, emboldens my vision, shapes my thinking, and gives trajectory to my calling.

The passage is from the January 6 entry, "Worship," based on Genesis 12:8. The whole entry is probably necessary for its fullest exposition, but the opening lines of the second paragraph serve as a summary: "Bethel is the symbol of communion with God; Ai is the symbol of the world. Abraham pitched his tent between the two."

Chambers explains,

> We have to pitch our tents where we shall always have quiet times with God, however noisy our times with the world may be. There are not three stages in spiritual life—worship, waiting and work. Some of us go in jumps like spiritual frogs; we jump from worship to waiting, and from waiting to work. God's idea is that the three should go together. They were always together in the life of Our Lord. He was unhasting and unresting. It is a discipline; we cannot get into it all at once.

When I first read that passage so many years ago, I was struck by the rare wisdom it contained. Indeed, after all this time, it remains rare wisdom. Finding a proper balance between heavenly concerns and earthly responsibilities is never easy. We are all constantly tugged between piety and practicality, between devotion and duty, between communion with God and calling in the world. Like tending a well-groomed garden, honing a balanced biblical worldview involves both the drudgery of daily labor and the high ideals of faith, hope, and love.

To "pitch our tents between Bethel and Ai" is such a profound way of describing our call to be *in* the world but not *of* it, to never quite be home until we're all the way home, to never bifurcate or dichotomize our callings into upper-story leaps or lower-story slumps. It is the perfect metaphor for describing a genuinely biblical worldview.

The truth is, a Christian view of the world and the things of the world is fraught with evident paradox—an appreciation for both the potentialities and the liabilities of fallen creation.

We know for instance, that the world is only a temporary dwelling place. It will "pass away" (1 John 2:17), and we are here but for a little while as "strangers" (Acts 7:6). Because we are a part "of [God's] household" (Ephesians 2:19), our true "citizenship is in heaven" (Philippians 3:20). Our affections are naturally set "on things above" (Colossians 3:2).

In addition, the world is filled with "hidden snares" (Jeremiah 18:22). In tandem with our sinful desires, it wages war against our souls (1 Peter 2:11). "Everything in the world—the lust of the flesh, the lust of the eyes, and the pride of life—comes not from the Father" (1 John 2:16). The world "cannot accept" the Spirit of Truth (John 14:17) because "the worries of this life and the deceitfulness of wealth choke the word, making it unfruitful" (Matthew 13:22).

Thankfully, Christ has "overcome the world" (John 16:33) and chosen us out of the world (John 15:19). Thus, we are not to "conform to the pattern of this world" (Romans 12:2), neither are we to "love the world" (1 John 2:15)—because Christ "gave himself for our sins to rescue us from the present evil age" (Galatians 1:4). Though we once "followed the ways of this world" (Ephesians 2:2), we now are to keep ourselves "from being polluted by the world" (James 1:27). Indeed, "friendship with the world means enmity against God," so that whoever is "a friend of the world becomes an enemy of God" (James 4:4).

Thus, warnings against worldliness, carnal mindedness, and earthly attachments dominate biblical ethics. In his book *Biblical Ethics*, Chambers said, "The counsel of the Spirit of God to the saints is that they must allow nothing worldly in themselves while living among the worldly in the world."

But then, that is the problem, isn't it? We must continue to live in the world. We must be "in" it but not "of" it. And that is no easy feat. As John Calvin says in the *Golden Booklet of the True Christian Life*, "Nothing is more difficult than to forsake all carnal thoughts, to subdue and renounce our false appetites, and to devote ourselves to God and our brethren, and to live the life of angels in a world of corruption."[1]

To make matters even more complex, we not only have to live in this dangerous, fallen world, but we have to work in it (1 Thessalonians 4:11), serve in it (Luke 22:26), and minister in it (2 Timothy 4:5). We have been appointed ambassadors to it (2 Corinthians 5:20), priests for it (1 Peter 2:9), and witnesses in it (Matthew 24:14). We even have to go to "the ends of the earth" (Acts 1:8), offering "a good confession" of the eternal life to which we were called (1 Timothy 6:12).

The reason for this seemingly contradictory state of affairs—enmity with the world on the one hand, responsibility to it on the other—is simply that "God so loved the world that he gave his one and only Son" (John 3:16). Though the world is "under the control of the evil one" (1 John 5:19) and "did not know" God (1 Corinthians 1:21), God is "reconciling the world to himself in Christ" (2 Corinthians 5:19). Jesus is

---

1. John Calvin, *Golden Booklet of the True Christian Life* (Grand Rapids, MI: Baker, 1952), p. 26.

"the light of the world" (John 8:12). He is the "Savior of the world" (John 4:42). He is "the Lamb of God, who takes away the sin of the world" (John 1:29). Indeed, He was made "the atoning sacrifice for our sins, and not only for ours but also for the sins of the whole world" (1 John 2:2). Through Christ, God will "reconcile to himself all things" (Colossians 1:20) so that finally "the kingdom of the world [will] become the kingdom of our Lord and of his Messiah" (Revelation 11:15).

A genuinely integrated Christian worldview must be cognizant of both perspectives of the world—and treat them with equal weight. It must be engaged in the world. It must be unengaged in worldliness. It must somehow correlate spiritual concerns with temporal concerns. It must coalesce heavenly hope and landed life. It must coordinate heartfelt faith and down-to-earth practice.

And that is just what Chambers had in mind when he charged us, like Abraham, to "pitch our tents" between Bethel and Ai. A vision of life and faith that is both unhasting and unresting, that has ready access to both the busy, noisy world and the quiet refreshment of heaven will enable us to walk in the midst of this poor, fallen world, fully invested in our daily callings yet with our eyes firmly fixed on the prize of eternity. Our sojourn between Bethel and Ai enables us to fulfill our responsibilities here without out ever being altogether at home. Thus, the high ideals of a biblical worldview are happily instituted by the grace of God in our lives, our work, and our ministries.

Between Bethel and Ai—that is where I pray the Lord would enable me to pitch my tents, until that glorious day when I am brought all the way home, where tents will be exchanged for mansions. Oh, how grateful I am that Oswald Chambers was able to articulate so clearly this balanced vision of what it means to be "in the world, but not of it."

 George Grant is the pastor of Parish Presbyterian Church (PCA); the founder of Franklin Classical School, the Chalmers Fund, and the King's Meadow Study Center; and the author of more than five dozen books. He served as an assistant to D. James Kennedy at the Coral Ridge Presbyterian Church and taught at Knox Theological Seminary. He makes his home in Middle Tennessee, near the historic town of Franklin, with his wife and coauthor, Karen. Together they have three grown children and four grandchildren.

AMBER LIA

Why shouldn't we go through heartbreaks?
Through these doorways God is
opening up ways of fellowship with His Son.
NOVEMBER 1, "YE ARE NOT YOUR OWN"

In the predawn fog I made my way down the hills of my college campus, lugging my duffel bag and running shoes. The
shuttle bus thrummed quietly in the dark, waiting for the
athletes to board. I made my way toward the back and sank
into my seat. Across the center aisle, my teammate Katherine
raised her head. I intended to greet her with a smile but her
tears stopped me.

"Katherine, are you okay?" My voice wavered with concern.

"I will be," she murmured.

I quickly moved across the aisle to simply sit beside her,
knowing that the presence of a friend was often more com-
forting than words.

Other members of our cross-country team trickled down
from the dorm rooms and filled the seats around us as we
prepared to leave for a race. Coach consulted his roster and
before long, we were on our way. Down the road a ways,

Katherine handed me the little book she had been clasping to her chest like a security blanket. It was a worn copy of *My Utmost for His Highest* by Oswald Chambers.

"I read this when I woke up this morning," she said, breathing a sorrowful yet strangely peace-filled sigh. "My fiancé ended our engagement last night. God knew I needed to hear these words today."

I thumbed to the day's date, November 1, and began reading. As I neared the end of the poignant devotional, I was struck by Oswald Chambers's charge to the brokenhearted:

> Why shouldn't we go through heartbreaks? Through those doorways God is opening up ways of fellowship with His Son. Most of us fall and collapse at the first grip of pain; we sit down on the threshold of God's purpose and die away of self-pity, and all so-called Christian sympathy will aid us to our death-bed. But God will not. He comes with the grip of the pierced hand of His Son, and says—"Enter into fellowship with Me; arise and shine." If through a broken heart God can bring His purposes to pass in the world, then thank Him for breaking your heart.

Katherine, in the midst of her shattered dreams was yielding, even then, to God's purposes in her life. Her broken heart was the "thoroughfare" Chambers describes as the pathway to entering into the fellowship of Jesus Christ's sufferings.

As I read my own copy of *My Utmost for His Highest* over the years, little did I know that that this devotional would be one I would memorize, out of sheer desperation.

Like many young people, I felt that my college days were the launching pad for some grandiose life plans. In the years after graduation, I was living on a high—teaching at a wonderful school, enjoying solid friendships, and hoping that one day in the near future, I would marry and have children. But the fragile bubble of the good life encased me in a sense of false security. Though I loved God and was being used by Him to reach my students, I had some refining to go through.

I watched as, one by one, my childhood friends and my college classmates married. As they entered into parenthood, our relationships began to change—and our lives slowly and naturally began to drift apart. Years of singleness allowed me to minister to my students, but my desire for companionship —to be a wife and mother—left me questioning God. My heart was not fully surrendered to His will, and that stole my joy more than I cared to admit.

And then, it was my turn. I met the man I was going to marry, the one I would build a comfortable life with "till death do us part."

My mother and I spent months in a whirlwind of joyful wedding planning. I chose a designer dress, seasonal flowers, and a quaint venue. We sampled shrimp hors d'oeuvres and passion fruit cake. My fiancé designed my wedding ring and the cushion cut sparkler fit like a dream on my finger.

Everything was falling into place until everything fell apart.

I had waited for so long to be married that I never imagined God would allow my own broken engagement. And not once, but twice. I lost money, friends, dreams, and in some ways, my faith. I spent my nights in tears, and my mornings in tears. I lamented with the psalmist and wondered if God could see me in my distress. Each day, I desperately pleaded with God for comfort. As November 1 approached, I turned to my tried-and-true Chambers's devotional.

The opening verse, 1 Corinthians 6:9, said, "Know ye not that . . . ye are not your own?"

I continued reading:

There is no such thing as a private life—"a world within the world"—for a man or woman who is brought into fellowship with Christ's sufferings. God breaks up the private life of His saints, and makes it a thoroughfare for the world on the one hand and for Himself on the other. No human being can stand that unless he is identified with Jesus Christ. We are not sanctified for ourselves, we are called into the fellowship of the Gospel, and things happen which have nothing to do with us, God is getting us into fellowship with Himself. Let Him have His way, if you do not, instead of being of the slightest use to God in His Redemptive work in the world, you will be a hindrance and a clog.

That day on the shuttle bus in college came sharply into focus. I remembered Katherine's grief mingled with hope. In the months following her loss, she continued to trust the Lord, and I knew that I needed to do that as well. My circumstances could not be the source of my happiness or joy. As I clung to the Word of God I found comfort in Psalm 52:8–9:

> But I am like an olive tree
>   flourishing in the house of God;
> I trust in God's unfailing love
>   for ever and ever.
> For what you have done I will always praise you
>   in the presence of your faithful people.
> And I will hope in your name,
>   for your name is good.

Eventually, the Lord blessed me with a wonderful husband and the children I longed for, but that was never His end goal. As Chambers said, God wants us on "rugged Reality until we do not care what becomes of us individually as long as He gets His way for the purpose of His Redemption."

The prescription for healing my broken heart was surrendering to God for His lofty purposes. The administration of such a holy tonic required that I praise Him in the middle of my angst. I had no desire to be a hindrance and a clog.

That cool November day, I thanked God for breaking my heart. I would thank Him again years later as I bent over the casket of a young cousin lost to breast cancer. And again when my fourth pregnancy ended in the miscarriage of my twin babies. I would learn to thank God for breaking my heart over the chronic illness of my son, persecution from family over my beliefs, and the loss of my husband's job. Each of the fragmented portions of my heart stirred within me a renewed sense of humility, a compassion for others, and an eternal hope that could not be easily dashed.

My life—your life—belongs to Jesus; we are bought with a price, and when we yield to Him, we receive the better end of the deal.

Trials are a result of living in a fallen world. Satan would have us buckle under the weight of our sorrows and tests, but he doesn't have to succeed in his plan to destroy us in our grief. Jesus came to offer us life to the full. The full life flows from a heart made whole not by achieving every whim and desire, but by the beautiful scars of a man or woman yielded to the purposes of God. Oswald Chambers knew this well, and I will always be grateful for his example.

 A former high school English teacher and the best-selling author of *Triggers: Exchanging Parents' Angry Reactions for Gentle Biblical Responses*, Amber Lia is a work-at-home mom of four boys under the age of ten. She and her husband, Guy, own Storehouse Media Group, a faith-friendly and family-friendly TV and film production company in Los Angeles, California. You can find Amber writing to encourage families on her blog *Mother of Knights* (motherofknights.com).

ERIN STRAZA

*Naturally, we are inclined to be so mathematical
and calculating that we look upon uncertainty
as a bad thing. We imagine that we have to reach
some end, but that is not the nature of spiritual life.*
APRIL 29, "THE GRACIOUSNESS OF UNCERTAINTY"

Something is different now, twenty-plus years since I first met Jesus.

Back then, in the first-love period, everything about God was new to me. I met Jesus when I was a senior in high school, after a childhood of longing after God. My church background was limited, but I had a Good News Bible that I cracked open periodically in an attempt to draw near to the God I knew existed but always seemed to miss. But one summer morning, the weight of my need for forgiveness intersected with a dawning of God's grace. Jesus closed the spiritual gap and reconciled me to the Father. The God I had desperately wanted to know had been longing for me, too.

My rescue from sin and sadness brought immediate and evident changes. Long-bound places in my heart and soul broke wide open. Jesus set me free, indeed, with a freedom that was palpable. Scripture was the feast where I consumed the history, the songs, the parables, and the epistles related to my heavenly citizenship. All of it was new, much of it confusing; my understanding was dim at best. Still, my heart would burn with joy over the great mystery of the God who had found me.

What I didn't understand didn't disturb me then; I knew God loved me and that Jesus had died to set me free. Within that beautiful truth, all other mysteries were held in trust.

It wasn't long afterward that I discovered *My Utmost for His Highest*. Oswald Chambers became a spiritual mentor of sorts, teaching me to pursue this mysterious God with everything in me. The pursuit was key, even more so than the discovery—for there would ever be more unknowns of our boundless God. There was good in the seeking, and curiosity wrapped in trust allowed me to pursue Jesus without needing to know it all or figure everything out.

But somewhere along the way, things changed. My pursuit of God became a pursuit of knowing things about God. I lost my wonder of God himself, getting lost in the categorization of thoughts and theories. I don't know when it happened, exactly. I'm guessing it was bit by bit as I discovered other books and thinkers and gained familiarity with the previously unfamiliar vocabulary of theology.

I'd also discovered that there are not just simply Christians and non-Christians—there are certain *types* of Christians. And each type gathers unto its own, forming theological camps with marked boundary lines and shared norms. Suddenly my eyes were wide-open to skirmishes and debates I once had no knowledge of. Within the fray, I tried to understand the differences to determine which side of each line I should stand on. I wanted to figure out the camp in which I fit so I could gain a certainty of place and person.

More than twenty years later, I'm still not sure if I've

pitched my tent in the right spot, if I've followed the right thinker. Basking in the unknown isn't something that comes naturally to the human soul—we prefer to *know*. We don't want to be caught off-guard. We want to know who's with us, and who's not. And so the theological camps slice and dice the mystery until we're left with a ragged mess. The resulting burden of worry is a thief of our spiritual wonder.

Despite the stifling of my curiosity, God's Spirit would regularly draw me away from the need to have everything figured out. Often I would feel a tug back to *My Utmost* and the simple yet timeless messages that inspired me to pursue God with my deepest passion.

The loss of wonder is addressed in the April 29 entry: "When we become advocates of a creed, something dies; we do not believe God, we only believe our belief about Him." Camp life did this to me. I traded the mystery of an all-powerful, beyond-comprehension God for a handful of camp-approved theologies and ideologies that could be more easily controlled, contained, and regulated.

The poet John Keats described a literary concept he called "negative capability." It's the idea that we must learn to live with the unsettling fact that some matters in life will never be fully understood, that much of life will be out of our control. True as it may be, I would guess his commentary was less than popular. Who wants to hear that life cannot be managed or understood?

In my early years as a Christian, my faith rested squarely on the Person of Jesus Christ. I was at home with negative capability because I knew God was the Great Unknown who loved me enough to claim me and call me His own. The things I didn't understand and couldn't manage were of little consequence: God had my back, so I was at peace.

But years later, negative capability had turned sour in

my heart. I distanced myself from the unknown because, as I moved about various Christian circles, I didn't want to look ignorant. Keeping up appearances is wearying work, though—work for which I could no longer muster energy once my life circumstances turned a bit dark. More than anything else, I wanted to return to my first love. It was time to put aside the need for camp approval and endorsement. A desire to appease men over God was (and has continued to be) the wake-up call I needed.

Turning away from old things is part and parcel of spiritual maturity. Ongoing spiritual formation is marked by putting off life-draining ways to then embrace life-giving ones. Each time I am prompted to put off elements of the old self, I turn to *My Utmost*, for in it, Chambers points me to a life that is certain about one thing: God. Being certain, in and of itself, is not problematic; rather, it's the object of my certitude that matters. Placing certainty in anything other than God will shrink my perception of Him. It will fool me into thinking I can eliminate the uncertainties that come from being a creature in the Creator's world.

Key to living with negative capability is a childlike trust in God. Children are often obliviously at rest in the care and provision of their parents. But with regard to faith, trust is not a state of ignorance—it is not the absence of the unknown but rather the ability to accept what we don't know. Jesus explained,

> "Truly, I say to you, unless you turn and become like children, you will never enter the kingdom of heaven. Whoever humbles himself like this child is the greatest in the kingdom of heaven."   —MATTHEW 18:3–4 ESV

The spiritually mature are not the camp gatekeepers, but those with childlike faith. Faith allows us to live with the unknown because we know the God who knows all. Choosing to humble myself before God means that I give up everything I *think* I know about Him and the world. This is no small thing.

Thought leaders of faith today have almost unlimited opportunities to proclaim their particular –ologies to the masses. But Chambers warns, "The nature of spiritual life is that we are certain in our uncertainty, consequently we do not make our nests anywhere."

The spiritual life is the one Chambers speaks of throughout *My Utmost*. It is the one laden with possibilities and "what ifs." This is the life where God shows up in unexpected, surprising ways. This is when we encounter Jesus himself, the One who is beyond comprehension.

How grateful I am that Jesus continues to call me to His side, not to a particular camp. He doesn't ask me to be certain of anything but His redeeming love. This is where I want to pitch my tent: right here, where uncertainty meets humility and mystery leads to wonder.

Erin Straza is managing editor for *Christ and Pop Culture*, host of the *Persuasion* podcast, and author of *Comfort Detox: Finding Freedom from Habits that Bind You*. As a freelance writer and communications consultant, Erin creates and edits content for various organizations, including Spread Truth, *Christianity Today*, American Farm Bureau, and Dunham + Company. Erin lives in the Illinois flatlands with her husband, Mike.

SHELLY MILLER

If our hopes seem to be experiencing
disappointment right now,
it simply means that they are being purified.
FEBRUARY 22, "THE DISCIPLINE OF SPIRITUAL PERSEVERANCE"
(UPDATED EDITION)

Walking back into the bedroom after a brief time of morning prayer, I found my husband sliding his feet through his pant legs. H (that's his whole name) shuddered upon my entrance. He isn't skittish, so the reaction stopped me in my tracks.

It was a Monday, but he wasn't getting ready for work. He was deep in thought, preparing prayerfully for an imminent Skype chat with two leaders in London—people responsible for the jobs that allowed us to live in England on a visa. Several months earlier, H had resigned from a beloved, high-level position with a church planting movement in order to fulfill a Macedonian call to the British capital.

What we assumed would be a seamless transition mutated into a lengthy, bureaucratic muddle. "A few months" to make a move had become a few seasons on the calendar. His eyes told me he was weary from waiting, wanting to be strong but feeling vulnerable (as I was) after the loss of a sale on our house that week. It felt like three steps forward, two steps back when we had assumed we were already on the back side of the mountain we'd been climbing for months.

Our assurance about our decision to move to London came from a track record of God's faithfulness over twenty-six years of marriage and ministry together. We were certain that He was leading us, not because the details were falling into place but because we had learned to distinguish His loving whispers from the voice of selfish ambition. Previously, in similar situations, God had highlighted the transition with hints of confirmation, a grace allowing us to endure despite opposition. But this time, the signs were not as obvious, making the map we'd used in the past obsolete. We began questioning our ability to navigate altogether. This loss of security in predictable patterns allowed us to begin living out Oswald Chambers's definition of perseverance.

In the February 22 entry of the updated edition of *My Utmost for His Highest*, perseverance is described as "more than endurance. It is endurance combined with absolute assurance and certainty that what we are looking for is going to happen. Perseverance means more than just hanging on, which may be only exposing our fear of letting go and falling."

As H buttoned his shirt, a television news report captured both of our attention. We heard a story about two US climbers that illustrated Chambers's words quite literally, bringing us consolation.

Kevin Jorgeson and Tommy Caldwell were interviewed after conquering the face of El Capitan in Yosemite National Park. Their fingers were cracked with fissures, raw and bleeding. During the climb they slept on flat pieces of rock under tents, harnessed with ropes to prevent a deadly fall. After two weeks, they were weary, and admitted that their resolve waned under the harsh conditions. Yet they reached the summit of the 3,000-foot (914m) rock. They made history as the first climbers to do so without aids.

I couldn't help but see their climb as a metaphor for our waiting season, a parallel in our race of perseverance. When the pain of circumstances caused our trust in God's ways to wane, I wanted to give up and slide down the safety rope, back to the comfortable and familiar. But in my heart, I knew we were nearly there. I knew that we needed to persevere, trusting in Jesus for rescue, "refusing to believe that our hero is going to be conquered," as Chambers said (updated edition).

But H and I weren't the only ones waiting. Our two teenage kids waited with us, too. When life became weighty and unmanageable, would they witness their parents' longing to slide back, into predictable rhythms of work or some familiar behavior to ease the discomfort? Oddly, it is often easier to accept a bad resolution than to live in a constant state of uncertainty.

During the excruciating silence of this season, we began repeating a question during times of prayer: "What do you want us to do?" And the longer we agonized over the lack of concrete solutions, that question eventually became a desperate plea: "We'll do anything you ask, just tell us what to do." What we discerned God saying back to us did not tickle our ears: "I don't want you to *do* anything, I want you to *be* with Me."

The initial bravery we felt when we left comfort and security to accept a ministry call to London had been compromised—because God wasn't providing a way forward in the same way He had with eight previous moves throughout our marriage. We began to experience the fear Chambers spoke of, "that the very things our Lord stood for—love, justice, forgiveness, and kindness among men—will not win out in the end and will represent an unattainable goal for us."

We feared that God was making this chapter of our story a humorous tale to be repeated as folklore by future generations. We feared disappointing our children and missing God's best. Personally, I feared God was not the Father I had envisioned after decades of following Him. I wrongly equated His silence with ambivalence—or worse, a mean-spirited response based on my inability to somehow measure up to His standards.

But I would learn later that while God wasn't giving me what I wanted, He was giving me what I *needed*. He was giving me himself, the ultimate act of love. It became clear that my need for certainty had become an idol. With the ugly revelation that I desired security in the unknowns more than I wanted a Savior, I knew what Chambers refers to as "the call to spiritual perseverance" was a choice I had to make. It was "a call not to hang on and do nothing, but to work deliberately, knowing with certainty that God will never be defeated."

For us, spiritual perseverance began to look like taking the fourth commandment more seriously: "Remember the Sabbath" (Exodus 20:8). We needed the deliberate act of making rest the axis of our days while consciously believing His plans for us were good—despite the anxiety we felt. "Rest" in this case wasn't just napping on the couch; we were letting go of our need for concrete details and surrendering our ability to plan for the future. We were resting in our Father's love while packing moving boxes, knowing that His timing is perfect and His highest aim is to bless us. We found peace is a Person and not a place.

The February 22 entry of *My Utmost* begins with Psalm 46:10, "Be still, and know that I am God." This verse is not as much about meditation as it is about the intervention of God's kingdom here on earth. "Be still," from the Hebrew term *raphe*, means to be weak, to let go, to release. But in Hebrew grammar, the emphasis is on the second imperative, "know." We surrender our timetables, let go of our preferred outcomes, and die to the god we create in our own image in order to fully *know* the King of Kings and Lord of Lords. Once we give up our self-sufficiency and trust in God's all-sufficiency, joy and awe replace anxious desperation. We can persevere because we know He controls all the details of our future.

The uncertainties of life are sure to disappoint and discourage us, clouding our judgement. The command to "be still and know that I am God" reminds us that we are finite and He is infinite. While our own weariness can cause a subtle negotiation with truth, rest confronts the lies we tell ourselves. This is the good news in perseverance.

After we watched the news report on the climbers, H wrapped his arms around me, leaning back to look into my eyes. I told him I'd been praying, and explained an impression I'd had during my prayer time. "I had that same impression in my prayers this morning," he responded.

Two hours later, H was in the family room on his call while I paced in the next room, silently reciting the character of God, as revealed in the Psalms, back to Him. Nervous energy pulsed through my body, making sweat rings under the arms of my shirt. But soon, H walked into the room smiling, relieved, and happy. Though there would be more paperwork and waiting ahead, he had met the final requirement in a sponsorship process that allowed us to receive a visa to live in England.

There are times when we are tempted to view hardship and stress as a cue to give up hope, to grieve the loss of a dream. Instead of choosing rest, our natural inclination is to *do* something, anything, to limit the pain, change unwanted circumstances, and resolve difficulties. Some of our immediate reactions are appropriate, but God always tells us to "remember" and "be still."

Don't just endure because you are afraid of failing—persevere because God's love prevails. "He brings fulfillment," Chambers says, "'because you have kept My command to persevere' (Revelation 3:10)."

Shelly Miller is a veteran ministry leader and founded the Sabbath Society, an online community of people who want to make rest a priority. She is the author of *Rhythms of Rest: Finding the Spirit of Sabbath in a Busy World*. Her writing has been featured in publications internationally and she speaks in venues around the world. Shelly and her husband, H, live as expats in London, England, where they help resource church planting efforts. They are parents of two children, Murielle and Harrison. Find more of Shelly's writing at ShellyMillerWriter.com.

JED AND CECILIE MACOSKO

We are so abominably serious,
so desperately interested in our own characters,
that we refuse to behave like Christians
in the shallow concerns of life.
November 22, "Shallow and Profound"

If you read *My Utmost for His Highest,* you are serious about your relationship with God. It's hard work to understand expressions like the "retired sphere of the leasts" (April 19) and other mind-bending sections of *Utmost.* So making the time and effort to read Oswald Chambers's deep wisdom is a sign that you take your walk with God seriously.

So far so good. But what if we take *ourselves* seriously?

When we take ourselves seriously, we risk being the very reason some people hate going to church, loathe attending Christian-sponsored events, and despise spending time with "born again" believers. We risk being more focused on impressing people than on enjoying God. No one wants to be around that!

Thankfully, Oswald and Biddy Chambers were well aware of our tendency to take ourselves seriously. The November 22 *Utmost* devotional warns us not to refuse the shallow things of life, since shallow things are what keep us from taking ourselves too seriously. Here's what it says:

> Beware of allowing yourself to think that the shallow concerns of life are not ordained of God. . . . It is not your devotion to God that makes you refuse to be shallow, but your wish to impress other people. . . . The shallow amenities of life, eating and drinking, walking and talking, are all ordained by God. . . . Our safeguard is in the shallow things.

So "shallow things" are things like eating and drinking, walking and talking. In our time, these things would be considered the everyday activities of life—so we will use the expression "everyday activities" to keep things clear.

Everyday activities guard us as we live out the life of Christ. Without everyday activities, we wouldn't notice that the Spirit of Christ is working miraculously through us. On the flip side, everyday activities show us what parts of our life we are trying to keep separate from God. They function as a wake-up call for people who think they already are Christians but aren't—for example, people who go to church every Sunday and believe all the right things but who don't have the life of Christ in them. In this case, everyday activities could safeguard these people from an eternity apart from God!

Often, there are four stages to our everyday experience. The first stage is failure. Before we became Christians, we may have not failed in our everyday activities as obviously as we do now. Why is that? Oswald Chambers tells us it's because God is not interested in making us into "specimens of holiness to put in His museum" (December 2). God wants to develop a closeness with us, and one way He builds closeness is by getting us to the point where we can trust nothing else but Him. God will put us into everyday situations where we fail miserably, and all our powers and skills are proven to be absolutely untrustworthy.

After we fail, we move to the second stage of everyday experience: wallowing in self-pity. We might realize that we were trusting in the wrong thing, but we don't yet put our trust in God. Instead, we feel depressed and sorry that our powers and skills failed us. In the middle of all this self-pity, God sends us an everyday activity that once again acts as our safeguard. As we go about doing this everyday activity, our self-pity takes a back seat to whatever it is we're doing. This is a good thing, and it leads us to the next stage of God revealing the life of Christ in us.

The third stage is when we face a new challenge in our everyday activities. As the life of Christ—in other words, the Holy Spirit—takes more control of our life, we see that our failure is not quite as miserable. Sometimes, when faced with that new situation, we don't fail at all. As the updated edition of the March 23 devotional says:

> What is the proof that carnality has gone? . . . God will see to it that you have a number of opportunities to prove to yourself the miracle of His grace. The proof is in a very practical test. You will find yourself saying, "If this had happened before, I would have had the spirit of resentment!" And you will never cease to be the most amazed person on earth at what God has done for you on the inside.

Our "carnality" is our tendency to live the old life of the flesh, not the new life of Christ. When God reveals the life of Christ in us and shows that our carnality is gone, He does it by giving us a practical, everyday kind of test. By reacting to this test in a new way, without the old resentment, we know for sure that the life of Christ is within us.

The fourth and final stage of experience is when we go about our everyday activities with the joy of closeness with God, through the life of Christ inside us. This seems to be the way Oswald lived much of his life: he romped on the floor with toddlers, took his hosts on sleigh rides, and celebrated Christmas with his friends in hearty laughter—even though they had to split a meal for two among three people! Chambers's life seemed to exude a constant joy, which flowed out of his closeness with God.

Well, then, how do everyday activities help us personally? Jed grew up in the church; Cecilie is an adult convert. For Jed, the idea of skipping Bible study, even to do a pleasant everyday activity like taking a walk or working in the garden, was out of the question. But thanks to Cecilie, who always loved walking and gardening, he has seen how a less-regimented approach to church, Bible study, and other public manifestations of Christianity can help put the kibosh on spiritual snobbery. By his own admission, he's still a spiritual snob—but at least he is aware of it now!

At times, Cecilie thinks she knows something, but just when she is fairly confident she has the details worked out, God sends an unexpected new situation that knocks down her carefully constructed ideas. This occurs in the "shallow" realm that Oswald talks about, a humbling but extremely necessary step in bringing her back into a closer relationship with God. And it almost always starts with a situation in everyday life, not with some deep theological concept.

When we wrote our study guide *A Daily Companion to My Utmost for His Highest*, we told our readers that if they didn't already have a favorite the November 22 devotional would be a good choice. Now, a few years later, we still think that's true.

If you're like most people, you need every safeguard you

can get to protect yourself against the cult of self-worship, the danger of being, in Oswald's phrase, "a spiritual prig." Doing mundane, shallow, everyday activities can keep you out of trouble, especially if you know that God designed them to provide a test of whether the Spirit of Christ is living in us.

To recap the process:

- First, we fail at our everyday activities.
- Then, in the midst of our pity party, an everyday activity gets us back on track.
- Next, we face a similar test and do a little (or a lot!) better, proving Christ is in us.
- Finally, we begin walking through each day's activities with the presence of Christ.

Our everyday activities comprise the only arena that shows Christ's life in us. And that's exactly the way God intended it. Don't refuse everyday activities. Don't refuse to be shallow. These "shallow," everyday things are what will keep you safe until God calls you home!

Jed and Cecilie Macosko are a husband-wife writing team juggling their parenting responsibilities and two careers—Jed is a physics professor and Cecilie is a family doctor. The Macoskos and their five young children make their home in North Carolina. They are the authors of *A Daily Companion to My Utmost for His Highest*. Audio files are available for free at www.lookingglasslearning.org.

SHEILA SEILER LAGRAND

Get into the habit of saying, "Speak, Lord,"
and life will become a romance.
JANUARY 30, "THE DILEMMA OF OBEDIENCE"

I settled my book on flower arranging into a wrought-iron cookbook stand, the pages open to the bouquet I was hoping to duplicate. But the effort wasn't going well. My Queen Anne's lace was stale and dropping petals. The tender aster stems were breaking. The blooms weren't completely hiding the foam that held the flowers.

Glancing at the clock, I saw I had ninety minutes to complete these two arrangements, then shower and dress for the memorial service for a friend's mother. It was a twenty-minute drive from the house, so I needed to allow travel time, too. Two teapots—one pink, one green, loaded with flowers I'd selected—were meant to be my gesture of sympathy and compassion to my friend. Unfortunately, the project was not coming together as I'd pictured it. Had my reach exceeded my grasp?

Fighting off a panic attack, I reread the appropriate section in my book. I began to think that maybe it had been a bad idea to try something new when I was on a schedule—and the results really mattered. I wondered if I should look for guidance in another book.

The clock was ticking. A tear of frustration glided down my cheek.

I muttered, "Good Father, dear Lord, I believe your word, that I will see your goodness in the land of the living. Could I see it right here in these flowers?"

Sure. Just start over.

I nearly dropped the teapot as I recognized the familiar resonance of God's voice.

Really. I've got this. Begin anew.

I quickly set fresh chunks of floral foam to soaking and rinsed the stems of the various flowers. Clearing off the mess I'd made during my first two attempts, I felt a bustling energy unfurling inside me as I closed the flower arranging book and picked up a pure white Asiatic lily. I inserted its stem into the foam. *Now a few roses.* Asters. Another lily. *Greenery— use those leaves you trimmed from the asters.*

At my urgent request, my husband had gone to the store to buy baby's breath, a replacement for that out-of-date Queen Anne's lace. By the time he arrived home, I'd arranged all the flowers for the first teapot and had nearly completed the second. I smiled at Rich and set down my floral shears. "It's okay," I said. "I've got it figured out. I got some help."

He looked both relieved and puzzled, as he had expected to find me tense and frustrated upon his return. "Help?" he asked.

I looked upward in a common, exaggerated gesture my husband understands. Rich grinned.

"Getting these flowers right is my heart's desire," I told him, referencing Psalm 37:4. "So I asked for the desire of my heart!"

That's not how I had always prayed. I used to reserve

prayer for life's really big crises: things like serious illness, family discord, and natural disasters sent me to my knees. But for the little things—stuff like my trouble with creating a few floral arrangements—I harbored the idea that I shouldn't "bother" God. Petty problems and trivial requests seemed out of line, and King David's words in 1 Chronicles 29:11 (NASB) resonated with me:

> "Yours, O LORD, is the greatness and the power and the glory and the victory and the majesty, indeed everything that is in the heavens and the earth; Yours is the dominion, O LORD, and You exalt Yourself as head over all."

So when I read in the January 30 entry of *My Utmost for His Highest*, "Get into the habit of saying, 'Speak, Lord,' and life will become a romance," I hit a mental speed bump. Frankly, nothing about my concept of a majestic, self-exalting God left room for "romance." That big, busy CEO of the universe occupied himself, I was certain, with the far more important matters of life, things like civil wars and babies with brain cancer—not my puny problems and shallow needs. And besides—isn't life with God all about sacrifice, self-denial, indeed *dying* to self so that Christ could dwell in me?

But my ruminations over this puzzling notion had distracted me from the first part of that sentence in *My Utmost*. Brother Chambers didn't write, "*Accept Jesus* and life will become a romance." No, he identified the *habit of asking God to speak* as what transforms life into a romance. Now, *romance* is a word that has always been fuzzily-defined for me, so I ventured to look up the meaning. The Oxford Dictionary defines it as "a feeling of excitement and mystery associated with love."

That did not align with the remote, omnipotent God I

had always imagined. Excitement? Mystery? *Love?* Those words belong to a personal, even intimate, relationship. They seem to describe a God who would lovingly tuck a morsel of bread into my mouth, not the God who multiplied a few small loaves of bread to feed five thousand sweaty strangers. Sure, they were beloved sweaty strangers (because, of course, God loves all people), but they were strangers just the same.

I sat there, pondering this apparent dissonance, when understanding overcame me like a tidal wave. After an instant of shock, I reclined into that wave—His loving, lifting, doting, merciful tidal wave—laughing aloud for the sheer joy of it.

I had wondered if I was worshipping a God of epic majesty or a God of tender, personal love. Oswald Chambers pointed me toward the answer when he said, "Every time circumstances press, say, 'Speak, Lord' [and] make time to listen. . . . As we listen, our ears get acute, and, like Jesus, we shall hear God all the time."

In another part of *My Utmost*, the February 13 entry, Chambers said, "The destiny of my spiritual life is such identification with Jesus Christ that I always hear God, and I know that God always hears me (John 11:41)."

When I picked up my Bible and said, "Speak, Lord," I read some other words of David: "As for me, I am poor and needy, but the Lord takes thought for me. You are my help and my deliverer; do not delay, O my God!" (Psalm 40:17 ESV).

Finally, I saw that my either-or question was foolish. *Because* of God's infinite might and knowledge, He cares for our measliest concerns. *Because* He conquered death, He can cool a fever. *Because* He placed the stars in the sky, He can guide a harried dad to the hiding place of his toddler's treasured bedtime blankie. *Because* He speaks over the roar of thunder, He can whisper directions to a budding florist.

Our God is a God of tender majesty and majestic tenderness. Only an infinite God would occupy himself with our most infinitesimal human petitions. Only a truly amazing God could hold two-way conversations with countless millions of people, turning life into "a romance," as Oswald Chambers would say.

Sheila Seiler Lagrand shares her home with her husband, Rich, and their three dogs. An anthropologist by training, her current projects include a book about grandparenting and another about recess—for adults. Her novel *Remembering for Ruth* released in November 2014. She enjoys writing, doodling, playing with flowers, and indulging her grandlittles. Find her at sheilalagrand.com.

ANNE MARIE MILLER

If you receive yourself in the fires of sorrow,
God will make you nourishment for other people.
JUNE 25, "RECEIVING ONE'S SELF IN THE FIRES OF SORROW"

"Do you want relief?" my friend Gail asked me. "Or do you want to be healed?"

Her words hurt my already vulnerable heart, but I knew she was right. There was a greater purpose to my grief . . . even if I didn't know it yet.

At the tender age of twenty-three, I had gotten married. Marriage, of course, is both rewarding and difficult. I was living life with my best friend—together we went on adventures, celebrated occasions with loved ones, and processed the loss of family members and friends. I never knew that a short few years later, I would grieve the death of my own marriage.

That seven-year relationship was a flag I waved loud and proud. I thought we were strong. I thought we were invincible. But only a month after our seventh anniversary, I received a phone call that would forever alter my life.

Nobody goes into a marriage thinking it will end, because what *you* have is different and special. You never would imagine a season when your body aches and you're desperate for the relief sleep brings because of all the weeping—weeping over the death of something so sacred, so familiar, so full of expectation.

If my marriage was a tree, I thought the roots were planted deep. Well nourished. Unmovable. Good roots bring life. But the thing about roots is that you can't see them. Sometimes they're not what you think, and death results. Until we are shocked by death, we rarely consider even the possibility of it.

My marriage, the tree I once revered as strong and unaffected, crashed to the ground. Until the day it happened, I thought we were among the strong trees, one of those that would grow tall and old and tell stories in quiet forests. But the roots weren't as deep as I perceived them to be. They hit rocks and bad soil that I didn't realize lay hidden below the surface. Without warning, the roots let go—and the impact of the fallen tree destroyed everything.

This was my crisis. For the first time in many years the left side of my bed was cold. The chest of drawers contained only my laundry, and the cup in the bathroom held only one toothbrush. I had two keys to one house, two keys to one car. The socks scattered on the floor were mine; no longer could I complain about his. If my marriage was a tree that crashed to the ground, the grief that followed was a forest fire that reduced to ashes everything I once cherished as dear and familiar.

Every year I've read Oswald Chambers's words in *My Utmost for His Highest*. Every year, his words of June 25 bypassed my life, which was mostly free from any large fires of suffering. But on this June 25, three days before the anniversary of my divorce, his words landed squarely on my heart: "If you receive yourself in the fires of sorrow, God will make you nourishment for other people."

Chambers built his thoughts around the words of Jesus in John 12:27–29, telling His disciples about His upcoming death: "What shall I say? Father, save me from this hour? But for this cause I came unto this hour. Father, glorify Thy name." What this means to us, Chambers taught, was that "my attitude as a saint to sorrow and difficulty is not to ask that they may be prevented, but to ask that I may preserve the self God created me to be through every fire of sorrow. Our Lord received Himself in the fire of sorrow, He was saved not *from* the hour, but *out of* the hour."

The year following my divorce was one of the most painful times in my life. To say I received the fires of sorrow is an understatement. I didn't really have a choice but to receive them—they consumed me. They burned up every bit of my identity as a woman, a wife, and even who I thought I was as a child of God. What was left among the ashes was proof that I worshipped my role as a wife more than I worshipped the one who had created me in His image.

My emotional and spiritual being turned to ash, and so did the more tangible things of life—my career and finances were scorched, never to be the same. At the age of thirty-one, I felt as if I had nothing to show for my thirteen years of adulthood. Everything I owned fit in my car. I had very little income because grief had thrown me into depression. Ultimately, I was hospitalized when I contemplated ending my life.

After my release, I was invited to live with some dear friends. They knew my need for a safe place, both physical and spiritual, and that is where the story turns. For it was in the living room of their home that my friend Gail asked me, "Do you want relief? Or do you want to be healed?"

At the time, I wanted relief. Another anniversary of the divorce was approaching and I wanted to avoid the day, to erase it from my calendar for good. I penned in my journal, "Will this day always be this painful?" I didn't just want relief—I craved it.

Then Gail's husband said, "This is the gospel made practical. Everyone wants the power of the Resurrection. Few are willing to endure the crucifixion to get there."

We love stories of restoration. But before freedom comes oppression; before redemption comes loss. We want to be rescued from our pain, now.

Do we know how to die, though? Are we willing to? Do we truly take on the form of Christ's sufferings, a suffering even to death?

I can never think of a time when I have prayed for sorrow or invited brokenness into my life. Usually, it comes as an unwelcomed guest. My prayer that night was one I would never have expected to pray. Praying for sorrow?

"Sorrow burns up a great amount of shallowness," Oswald Chambers taught. But, he said, "it does not always make a man better. Suffering either gives me my self or it destroys my self. You cannot receive your self in success, you lose your head; you cannot receive your self in monotony, you grouse. The way to find your self is in the fires of sorrow. Why it should be so is another matter, but that it is so is true in the Scriptures and in human experience."

The fires of sorrow bring us life. They can even bring us joy. I think the more refined we are through sorrow, the greater we are able to experience joy. And through that process, we take away an invaluable gift: empathy.

It's been almost ten years since my marriage ended. There is still pain, but I can honestly say I've been healed. Sadly, in the last several years, I've seen the fires of sorrow begin to consume other marriages around me.

Before my own divorce, I would have made assumptions,

saying I'd pray for the couples while my thoughts moved straight to judgment. Oswald Chambers recognized this tendency: "If a man has not been through the fires of sorrow, he is apt to be contemptuous, he has no time for you." But with the person who has "received himself" through the fires of sorrow, "you can go to him in trouble and find that he has ample leisure for you."

After my own fire, God's grace and glory has given me something others need: hope that there is healing and joy to be found, that they too may be able to pass along the gift of mercy.

As Oswald Chambers would say, "If you receive yourself in the fires of sorrow, God will make you nourishment for other people."

Anne Marie Miller is the author of five books that focus on mental, physical, spiritual, emotional, and sexual health. She has been in publications such as *Cosmopolitan*, *The New York Times*, *Publishers Weekly*, *Leadership Journal*, *Christianity Today*, and *Relevant*. She is in the process of becoming a nurse practitioner in geriatric psychiatry. Anne, her husband Tim, and her daughter Charlotte live in Texas.

JAMES HOSKINS

Drudgery is the touchstone of character.
The great hindrance in spiritual life is that we will
look for big things to do. "Jesus . . . took a towel, . . .
and began to wash the disciples' feet."
JUNE 15, "GET A MOVE ON"

One summer night when I was eighteen, my friends and I walked down a park trail. The only lights visible were the moon, the stars, and the soft glow of a cigarette dancing in front of me, held by a friend motioning with his hands, passionately explaining his philosophy of music.

We'd left a buddy's house earlier, deciding to take a walk and discuss the idea of starting a band together. For the others, the single fact that they wanted to play music was enough to say yes. But even though my desire to play was equally strong, that was not enough to make a decision. I needed a sign.

I felt paralyzed and indecisive—fearful of making the wrong choice. So I prayed silently to God, "If this is your will, show me." A few minutes later, I looked up just as a shooting star passed by. That sealed my answer: I was to have a career in music.

This pattern of decision making—looking for outward signs to tell me which choices to make—characterized most of my adolescence. Nothing scared me more than the thought of not "being in God's will."

Actually, there was something equally scary—the thought of a "normal" life filled with the mundane and void of any shooting-star experiences. I longed instead for a life of thrilling revelations and monumental accomplishments. I wanted to hear God's voice, to do big things for Him. The very idea of a routine, ordinary life made me uneasy, even depressed. I wanted to walk a path marked by signs and wonders, not the quiet, safe repetition of the everyday masses.

Growing up, certain things in my social environment added to these anxieties.

The first was my faith tradition: I was raised in a small Pentecostal church in the Midwestern United States where my dad was, and still is, the pastor. While I am thankful for the safe, loving environment our church provided, the wider culture around me—one of fiery youth conferences and revivals—taught me to value emotional experiences of God above all else. Determining God's will for my life meant constantly asking Him for a tangible sign or directive—apart from the occasional shooting star, that usually included things like a randomly chosen Bible verse taken out of context or a "prophetic word" just vague enough to read into it exactly what I wanted to hear. These "signs" sustained me in my Christian journey—I felt lost without them.

The second thing that fueled my anxiety over "normal" was the faithful hard work of my parents. Strange as it sounds, my parents' steady dedication to our family and the people in our church—a steadiness that I am now very grateful for—provided a baseline from which I wanted to individuate. Like many privileged, naïve young people, I thought becoming "my own person" necessarily meant being *different* from my parents. And since they were models of quiet Christian faithfulness in small things, I believed I was meant for *big* things.

My adolescent years waned, and my habit of decision-making (as well as the anxiety that fueled it) began to catch up with me. My music dreams didn't work out and neither did my next career choice, so I found myself angry with God, unable to deal with the mundane routine of my job. All the signs that I thought indicated God had "big plans" for me turned out to be wrong. And I found myself living the exact kind of normal life I had always dreaded.

It was at this point that a small, tattered devotional book—one my mom had given me in my early teens—would become a lifeline. I saw these words in the June 15 entry of *My Utmost for His Highest*:

> There are times when there is no illumination and no thrill, but just the daily round, the common task. Routine is God's way of saving us between our times of inspiration. Do not expect God always to give you His thrilling minutes, but learn to live in the domain of drudgery by the power of God.

For a young adult frustrated by his vocational circumstances, these words from Oswald Chambers represented a deep truth that my heart had always known on some level. But I had never been fully, consciously aware of it. Now, my frustration and resentment toward God began to slowly melt away. While I am still learning the truth of Oswald's words, on that day I discovered two important things about myself: I did not understand work, and I did not understand rest.

To that point in my life, none of my jobs were things I wanted to do or enjoyed doing. Instead, I saw them as necessary steps to get to what I *really* wanted to do, whatever that happened to be at the time. And what I really wanted to do, I also felt I *deserved* to do—that I could do nothing else. In a way, I resented the fact that I had to go through these preliminary steps to get to the goal.

Even worse, though I would never have admitted it, deep down I felt that God *owed it to me* to bring my career goals to fruition. After all, I had followed all of His rules, all of His "signs," working hard to get where I was—it was the least He could do.

That meant the motivation for my work—for my whole life, really—was the same as the people of Babel, "to make a name" for myself (Genesis 11:4). I was not working for God. I was not even living for Him, despite outward appearances. I was living and working to get what I wanted, what I felt I deserved—a comfortable life with the career of my dreams. God was just a means to reach that goal.

As a result, I was finding no joy or satisfaction in my work. No matter what job I had at the time, it always felt exhausting, unfair, and futile—even when it wasn't. And because of *that*, I never felt at rest, even if I was on holiday. I had no Sabbath.

So when I read Chambers's June 15 devotional, I felt a deep conviction in my spirit. It became clear to me that God had graciously provided these ordinary jobs not only for money and food, but for my salvation—to teach me how to be faithful to Him and to cleanse me of my pride and self-entitlement.

Slowly but surely, this new understanding began to change my daily practice. Instead of asking God to fulfill my long-term goals and dreams (or asking for a sign to affirm that He would), I would instead ask Him to help me do good work that day, to serve the people I would meet. I began to actually work for God instead of myself. And that changed *everything*.

Not only did my work become more satisfying and my rest more restful, I discovered it is possible to experience Sabbath rest *in* my work, even in a job I did not particularly enjoy.

Through my daily routine, I learned—I *am* learning—to surrender my fondest dreams to God and, whether He ever gives them to me or not, to love Him simply because He is worthy. And although signs are exciting encouragements that God sometimes gives, I'm also learning that He is sovereign even in the small, unexciting details of daily life. It is precisely these details—invisible, seemingly unimportant—that He grows and shapes into the big beautiful fireworks of His redemptive will. When our plans don't work out, His still do—and, thankfully, His plans are always better than ours.

So we can go about our lives confidently enjoying the present, being faithful in our daily tasks, not worrying about the future. We can walk our own path with the assurance that, signs or not, we are in His will. By doing so, we can discover (or rediscover) the truth of Oswald Chambers's words each day—"to live in the domain of drudgery by the power of God" and find that there is great joy in it.

Such a life, however "normal" it may appear, is supernaturally empowered—and therefore as exceptional and rare as any shooting star you may see.

James Hoskins is a teacher, writer, and musician. He has a B.A. in philosophy from the University of Missouri-Kansas City, and a M.A. in science and religion from Biola University. James writes about the intersection of reason, faith, and culture and is a contributor to *Christ and Pop Culture* and the *Christian Research Journal*. Find more of his writing and music at jameshoskins.net.

PHIL JOEL

For a while you say—
"I asked God to give me bread,
and He gave me a stone."
He did not, and to-day you find
He gave you the bread of life.
OCTOBER 11, "AFTER GOD'S SILENCE—WHAT?"

The best Christmas present my dad ever gave me came when I was seven years old. I'm guessing that he had an idea of what I wanted and may have somehow gotten me to confirm it without me even knowing. Whatever the case, he nailed it!

I remember tearing into the wrapping paper and catching my breath once I saw what lay beneath. It was a skateboard, but not just a regular board—this was a green Sims Viper! This was the board every kid in my neighborhood wanted but *I* got—me, a seven-year-old who didn't even ride standing up. (I would kneel on one leg and push with my other.) All the teenagers must have thought it was a mistake, or maybe that I'd borrowed or stolen it. I don't know if my dad knew how cool this thing made me feel, but it did. The Viper made me act like I owned the pavement.

Matthew 7:9 says, "Which of you, if his son asks for bread,

will give him a stone?" These words of Jesus make me think about my dad, about his heart to give his kids good things, because the Sims Viper skateboard was *way* more than I would have asked for or expected.

Now think about a child asking his parent for something he legitimately needs—food. And the parent responds not only by *not* providing him with that good and necessary thing, but by giving him something that is actually demoralizing—a stone. That would be pretty mean. It's almost unthinkable.

Not many parents are that cruel. Most would move heaven and earth to give their children everything they possibly can to make them healthy and strong. Most parents have a deep, abiding passion to provide for their precious children—even when they are less than lovable. We all know that kids can be disobedient, pushing every button, testing every boundary, and stretching their parents to the limits!

And that's *us* in our relationship to God. While we, as imperfect earthly parents, love and care for our children, God says His own father-heart for us far exceeds anything we could ever imagine (Ephesians 3:20–21).

But we don't always get what we ask Him to give us. Why?

In *My Utmost for His Highest*, Oswald Chambers spoke to those times that God is silent, when it seems like He isn't hearing our requests—or worse, giving us bad things instead of good. "For a while you say—'I asked God to give me bread, and He gave me a stone,'" Chambers says in the October 11 entry. "He did not, and to-day you find He gave you the bread of life."

It's hard to imagine the love our heavenly Father has for us because it far surpasses any love that we as limited, mortal beings are capable of. But it's something we really need to grasp, because when we understand the height, the depth, and the width of His love, it really does change everything—the way we feel about God and the way we live our lives. It's absolutely necessary to know the truth about God and how He feels about us. But first, let's look at some things that come against this truth.

Imagine a "spiritual" political campaign: Satan is running against God. Weapon of choice: Slander. Strategy: To get people to see God as the "mean guy"—the father who is silent, who doesn't listen, who doesn't have time; the one who is unloving, neglectful, easily angered; the one who, when His child asks for a piece of bread, gives him a stone.

Satan's campaign spends millions of dollars on propaganda that frames God as negatively as possible, all with the aim of changing people's core beliefs about Him.

Now, realize that this propaganda is *actually* happening . . . in real time. Satan's job is to twist the truth, slander God's character, and try to change our core beliefs about who He is and how He feels about us.

You may be falling for the propaganda if you wonder how God, your heavenly Father, sees you—or *if* He sees you. Is He listening? Does He love you? Even like you? Does He really care, or is that just something church people say because they're supposed to?

This world can get pretty noisy and complicated and confused, and it's easy to feel overlooked and forgotten—like you've gotten the raw end of the deal. No matter how many times you've asked God for things, He's handed you a "stone." If you were Satan, this is just the kind of thinking you'd want people to have—your campaign would be swinging in your favor.

I mention Satan's strategy only to recognize and uncover it. When we expose his tactics, people can see them for what they are—powerless lies. Now we need to look at the truth.

Oswald Chambers saw that God's silence is actually

something we are to be "trusted" with: "Are you mourning before God because you have not had an audible response? You will find that God has trusted you in the most intimate way possible, with an absolute silence, not of despair, but of pleasure, because He saw that you could stand a bigger revelation."

Silence is a form of grace, Chambers said, and "if Jesus Christ is bringing you into the understanding that prayer is for the glorifying of His Father, He will give you the first sign of His intimacy—silence."

The fact is that our heavenly Father is good—He is perfect in all His ways. He is deeply and desperately in love with each one of us! We are His, hand-crafted and knit together (Psalm 139:13). He's crazy about us—He knows every hair that's on our heads (Luke 12:7). He provides for our needs (Matthew 6:25–34). He loves us with the deepest love ever known—that of a parent to a child—even when we are less than lovable, even when we are disobedient, pushing every button, testing every boundary, and stretching Him to the limits!

That is the truth. But here's the deal—truth is only powerful when we choose to wear it like a belt (Ephesians 6:14). If we don't select the truth over the lies, it doesn't do us any good.

That's what I mean when I say that understanding the Father's love for us really changes everything. Our thinking moves from skepticism to wholehearted trust. Our poverty becomes "provided for." We go from unheard to listened to, misunderstood to understood by the very One who made us and is preparing an adventure for us. Lies tell us that times of silence mean God is turning away from us, but Chambers writes, "If God has given you a silence, praise Him, He is bringing you into the great run of His purposes."

We must consciously declare that God is good, that we are deeply loved by Him. When we remind ourselves of this great reality, our spiritual "ears" hear in the midst of the silence, and the truth sinks deeply into our hearts. Let's be people who stir ourselves with the facts of who our heavenly Father is as we choose to remember and declare them.

Even when He is silent, we can have confidence. As Oswald Chambers said, "A wonderful thing about God's silence is that the contagion of His stillness gets into you and you become perfectly confident—'I know God has heard me.' His silence is the proof that He has."

Phil Joel is best known for his long-standing role as bass player and vocalist for the multi-platinum-selling band Newsboys. Now he is the lead singer of Zealand Worship. Phil is married, and in 2005, he and his wife, Heather, began deliberatePeople, a ministry focused on communicating God's desire for us to live in true relationship—first with Him and then with those around us.

AMY BOUCHER PYE

Is my ear so keen to hear the tiniest whisper
of the Spirit that I know what I should do?
MAY 13, "THE HABIT OF A GOOD CONSCIENCE"

In a time of deep need in my twenties, I found myself
being discipled by some older, wiser mentors. One of them,
however, wasn't alive. But because of the wonderful editorial work of his wife, Oswald Chambers ministered to me
through his daily devotional, *My Utmost for His Highest*. The
Lord used this Scottish man who had lived decades before
to help me grow in my faith. In particular, Chambers taught
me to tune in to the words that God, through His Spirit, was
always speaking.

Growing up, I had been unsure of myself. I was a Minnesotan who later moved to the big city of Washington, DC,
with all of its exciting discussions and cultural happenings.
Although I donned a city wardrobe and learned to navigate the metropolis, at heart I remained one who lacked
confidence.

Perhaps subconsciously, I tried to find myself through
romantic relationships. But after a spectacular break-up,
viewing the scattered pieces of my life, I knew I needed a

better way. I wanted answers to the questions gnawing away inside me: Who am I? What do I really long for?

I scoured the Bible for its wisdom, ruminating on passages such as Psalm 63: "You, God, are my God, earnestly I seek you; I thirst for you, my whole being longs for you, in a dry and parched land where there is no water" (v. 1). Like King David, I felt parched for the living water that would fill my soul; I wanted to be "fully satisfied as with the richest of foods" (v. 5). I wanted to believe that God's love was better than life (v. 3).

When I had the opportunity to edit a book about listening to God, I started to find some answers. The author included the wisdom of Oswald Chambers as she revealed the exciting relationship between the disciple and her God. She knew a God of three persons—the Father, Son, and Holy Spirit—who was an active participant with her. She could hear God! I longed to hear Him too.

Oswald Chambers became a guide to finding this living Lord. As I read *My Utmost*, I met someone who saw God moving in his life. The Lord spoke to him. Chambers heard and obeyed the Lord and saw his prayers answered. I, too, wanted that kind of spiritual relationship.

One momentous morning I started to awaken to God's voice—and to His love—in a new way. As I meditated on the Scriptures, letting them sink into my heart, I sensed a still, small whisper from within yet seemingly outside me: "Beloved, I love you. And I lay my life down for you. Beloved, I died for you. You will find me when you seek me with all your heart. I have loved you with an everlasting love. I have called you by name."

Immediately I wondered, "Was that really God? Or was that just my own heart talking?" I tried to turn off my critical mind so that I could receive from God. For when I stilled myself, I heard this quiet voice saying that I was His beloved; that He loved me and would never leave me. That I was chosen and beautiful in His sight.

I recognized echoes of Scripture in these inner prompts: the Lord loving me with an "everlasting love" was from Jeremiah 31:3, and "You will seek me and find me when you seek me with all your heart" from Jeremiah 29:13. I started to let myself believe that the God of the universe was actually speaking to *me*; that He loved me everlastingly and that I was precious to Him. Day by day I began to experience what Chambers says in the January 30 entry of *My Utmost*, "Get into the habit of saying, 'Speak, Lord,' and life will become a romance." This romance was life-giving and life-changing—I would never be the same.

But I was on a journey, although I didn't realize it then. I rushed ahead with eager joy at words I thought were from the Lord. At times, in my enthusiasm, I got muddled up, thinking that God was speaking to me through His Spirit when actually it was my own heart and desires talking. God ultimately used a major disappointment in my life—the loss of both job and marriage opportunities in another city—to spur me to institute more rigorous means of testing what was and wasn't His voice.

My sadness over those losses, however, paled next to the sorrow I felt over not hearing God correctly. I had thought that He was ordaining the move, but it hadn't come to pass. What, I wondered, was I basing my life on? What was I listening to?

I needed to heed the wisdom of Chambers from that May 13 devotional:

> God always educates us down to the scruple. Is my ear so keen to hear the tiniest whisper of the Spirit that I know what I should do? "Grieve not the Holy Spirit." He does not come with a voice like thunder; His voice is so

gentle that it is easy to ignore it. The one thing that keeps the conscience sensitive to Him is the continual habit of being open to God on the inside.

The Lord was educating me through this grand disappointment. I thought His voice had been thundering out His directions for my life, directing me to move to that city and marry that man. Instead, I needed to discern the "tiniest whisper," something I could easily ignore. I needed to learn that God wanted me in a relationship of trust with Him, for He wanted me to develop the "continual habit of being open to [Him] on the inside." God didn't want to dictate my actions—He wanted me to step forth in faith, knowing that He was next to me and that I could collaborate with Him.

For a time, in my pain and disappointment, I gave up trying to discern the voice of God. I felt too hurt that I had been so wrong, and I didn't want to risk that again. But I missed my special communion with Jesus and the Spirit and the Father, the opportunity to pour out my feelings to Him and hear the loving words He sent in return.

Slowly, tentatively, over the period of many months, I started once again to share with the Lord what was on my heart and mind. I again embraced the "habit of being open to God on the inside." And when He would speak, I would listen, hoping that the voice really was God's.

This time I held the words tenderly, testing them against the wisdom of the Bible and sometimes sharing them with others who were mature in the Christian faith. I began to see that the romance of God's speaking could indeed be a daily reality, but that I needed to be open and humble. And as I walked with God, listening to and obeying Him, I found my deepest longings fulfilled by His love. The answer to that burning question of "Who am I?" was revealed, for I now knew with deep assurance that I was His beloved.

Maybe you've experienced something along the lines of my disappointment, when you thought you heard God but the promise didn't come to pass. If so, I encourage you gently not to give up on the practice of listening. For when we open our hearts and ears, the Lord *will* speak. He does that primarily through His Word, the Bible, but in our listening we may also hear the words of a hymn or a Spirit-inspired directive from a friend. That we sometimes hear things askew shouldn't prevent us from listening—we just need to be more vigorous in our testing.

As we hear God, we'll find that we flourish and grow, that we have received the strongest relationship that will fuel all of our others. As Oswald Chambers says in the January 7 entry of *My Utmost*, updated edition:

> Once we get intimate with Jesus we are never lonely and we never lack for understanding or compassion. We can continually pour our hearts to Him without being perceived as overly emotional or pitiful. . . . The picture resulting from such a life is that of the strong, calm balance that our Lord gives to those who are intimate with Him.

May it be so in our lives, to the glory of God.

Amy Boucher Pye is a writer and speaker who lives in North London. She's the author of the award-winning *Finding Myself in Britain: Our Search for Faith, Home, and True Identity* and *The Living Cross: Exploring God's Gift of Forgiveness and New Life*. She runs the Woman Alive book club in the UK and enjoys writing articles for *Our Daily Bread* and *Our Daily Journey*.

DAVID FREY

*God ventured His all in Jesus Christ to save us,
and now He wants us to venture our all
with total abandoned confidence in Him.*
MAY 8, "THE FAITH TO PERSEVERE" (UPDATED EDITION)

I am a coward. Most days I wrestle to find a reason to disrupt the empty bliss of comfortable. One such day in 2007, I had to make a decision to chase a dream or forever wonder what might have been.

I had an English education degree in hand, so why would I move to Nashville? Steady pay and a classroom full of eager minds sounded heavenly compared to the idea of relocating to the Music City. I had always lived happily in Indiana, surrounded by friends and family. Now I was going to travel the world with a band? I didn't even have prospective bandmates! When my buddy, Ben, suggested the move, it took true effort even to consider the notion of starting anew.

Once the leap was made, I found myself in a tiny room in a city I didn't know. I remember watching my parents drive away, and life instantly became both lonely and demanding. Gone were the college dorm days, with friends behind every door—days when true education mingled with the artificial security of federal loans that could be paid back in some other era. The contrasts were stark: chasing a dream looked like a used mattress, a rusty car, and piles of bills.

My first month in Nashville I felt like Frodo at the beginning of *The Lord of the Rings*: a young hobbit entrusted with the fate of the entire world facing insurmountable odds. "Impossible," the world would say. And if you had asked me for an honest appraisal of my chance of becoming a singer-songwriter, that's what I would have said.

But I truly believe that in that moment of my personal journey, though I was terrified and flooded with doubt, God began to write the next chapter of my life. He was smiling as I persevered.

I think of Job in the Old Testament. How did he proclaim, in all sincerity, "Though He slay me, yet will I trust Him" (Job 13:15 NKJV)? Oswald Chambers offers a possible answer in the May 8 entry of *My Utmost for His Highest* (updated edition):

> A saint's life is in the hands of God like a bow and arrow in the hands of an archer. God is aiming at something the saint cannot see, but our Lord continues to stretch and strain, and every once in a while the saint says, "I can't take it any more." Yet God pays no attention; He goes on stretching until His purpose is in sight, and then He lets the arrow fly.

How I wished then I could see what God had in store. How I wished I knew where I was going—but then life wouldn't require much faith.

It's the stretching that makes us strong enough to do all that God intends for us to do. In my own journey toward writing and singing the songs of my heart, there has been much stretching. My "help wanted" advertisement on Craigslist attracted bandmates who shared a common dream, but the road proved to be a constant source of distress. Though the book of James reminds us to "consider it pure joy, my brothers and sisters, whenever you face trials of many kinds" (James 1:2), the moment an actual trial begins is the moment I'm ready to quit.

Like that time the transmission of the band's van went out. Two months of shows at camps and churches through the Northeast had left us craving the hospitality of home. But our vehicle had given up on ever seeing home again. After a long run, the band was stranded, and I was feeling like *The Lord of the Rings* all over again. It was as if Frodo had finally achieved his goal, throwing the ring into the volcano and destroying evil, only to find that the rescuing eagles never showed up. No one wants to live in a volcano. We all want home.

So the band prayed for a way back. We persevered, and a friend found it in her heart to pay for a new transmission for our van. That might seem trivial in the grand scheme of world problems, but that one act of kindness allowed the Sidewalk Prophets to continue.

I love when God allows us to continue—He doesn't have to. That burned-out transmission could have spelled the end of my journey as a lead singer. We could have played our final show, but God saw the target that we could not.

Our friend's words, when she gave us the money for repairs, are dear to me: "I wish I could be in your shoes again," she said. "I miss taking those steps of faith. It demands real faith to do what you're doing."

The truth is, at the time I thought she was crazy. To *not* have risk or worry of the unknown every day would have been so much easier. I would have traded places with her right then and there—but like I said before, I am a coward.

Now that years have passed, her words are a constant encouragement. They're a reminder of where I've been, and a reminder to keep striving, to stretch what I believe is possible. They taught me that taking risks while aligning yourself to the will of Christ may leave you stranded, but you'll never be alone. As Oswald Chambers would say, "Even though you cannot see Him right now and cannot understand what He is doing, you know *Him*."

Late one night, not long after that transmission repair, I was asleep back home in Nashville. My phone woke me, and my mother was on the line, telling me I needed to hurry back to Indiana. My grandpa was dying.

I began to shake, afraid I wouldn't make it home in time to say good-bye. I was so startled by the news that I knew I couldn't drive, so I decided to sit down and write a letter to my granddad. It was a reminiscence about all the trips we had taken, all the joys he freely gave me, all the ways he reflected the love of Christ. I knew that that letter was more than just words on a page—it was a prayer. And even if I didn't make it home in time to read it to him, Grandpa knew those words by heart.

As soon as I finished writing, I grabbed my keys and drove through the night, making it to his bedside in time to say good-bye. I even read my grandpa the letter, worshiping with him one final time. Not many people get a chance to say their farewells—I consider myself incredibly blessed by the opportunity.

My grandpa was a great man. I can remember his words above everyone else's, compelling me to leave the comforts of home, to have courage, to chase a dream. He was a World

War II veteran who never lacked valor, leaving a legacy of faith. It is only appropriate that the first song our band released to radio was inspired by Grandpa's life, by the words that he would say to me.

Our band has now released four albums, toured the world, and seen thousands of lives saved by the love of Christ. I often wonder why God chose a coward like me to sing the songs He puts into my heart. I am so grateful for the faith He gave me to begin this journey, and I know I'll need to muster plenty of perseverance until the voyage is done. I have no idea what comes next—and I am grateful for that. If I knew it all, I'd somehow mess it up.

One day in April on the tour bus I found *My Utmost for His Highest*. I had been reading it most mornings, but out of my deep-seated pride I decided to skip ahead to my birthday's passage. On May 8, I would turn thirty-four. Thirty-four is so uneventful, I was a bit underwhelmed by life. But Oswald Chambers's words shook me:

> The real meaning of eternal life is a life that can face anything it has to face without wavering. If we will take this view, life will become one great romance—a glorious opportunity of seeing wonderful things all the time. God is disciplining us to get us into this central place of power.

How I long to hear God say those words of Revelation 3:10, the verse that precedes the *My Utmost* entry: "Because you have kept my command to persevere . . ."

Perseverance is a daily strife as well as a daily treasure. Faith is scary and oh so beautiful! I pray that my heart might "face anything it has to face without wavering"—so that life becomes "one great romance." Thank you, Lord, for this journey!

 David Frey is lead singer and founding member of the Dove Award–winning group Sidewalk Prophets. The band has been nominated for a Billboard Music Award, sold over 500,000 albums and 1.5 million digital singles, garnered five number one singles and eight top five radio hits, and played over 2,000 shows to 2.5 million fans. Sidewalk Prophets are known for spending the majority of their time touring and are passionate about connecting with their audience.

ADDIE ZIERMAN

God's purpose in the cloud is to simplify
our belief until our relationship
to Him is exactly that of a child—
God and my own soul.
July 29, "What Do You See in Your Clouds?"

In high school, I kept *My Utmost for His Highest* on my bed-side table alongside my journal and my heavily-underlined Teen Study Bible. The Bible was in a black carrying case with the words *Jesus Freak* stitched into the bottom corner. The journal was filled with quotes and prayers, feelings and faith declarations. Oswald Chambers's classic devotional was dog-eared and worn.

I didn't know anything about the "holiness movement" then—but it sure seemed to know about me. If it wasn't outright embraced in the evangelical '90s culture in which I came of age, it was certainly an undercurrent.

During those years, evangelicalism crackled with the notion of being "on fire for God"—a concept that sounded so *right* to my fifteen-year-old-heart . . . but that also required a certain amount of striving. Being "on fire" carried with it both an implied and an often explicit demand to throw into that flame anything that hindered—or could possibly, maybe, *eventually* hinder—your faith.

So I kissed dating good-bye and made Jesus my boyfriend. I got rid of my Mariah Carey *Music Box* CD and stocked my music collection instead with DC Talk and the Newsboys. I drew boxes around myself to keep myself from sin, and then I drew boxes around *those* boxes until I existed in a very small world built of Christian rock and Christian romance novels and Christian teen magazines.

"Holiness is what I long for," I sang in the church youth group worship band. "Holiness is what I need! Holiness is what you want from me." At age fifteen, arms raised, singing my heart out in the church gymnasium, I didn't really know what *holiness* meant. I had it confused with a kind of spiritual perfection, and that perfection is what I was reaching for when I stretched out my arms in worship every week.

It seemed to me a simple equation: *doing* things for God plus *sacrificing* things for God equaled *more God*. I imagined that if I fed enough of myself into the fire of my faith, it would burn bright and wild and incandescent forever.

What I didn't factor into my pretty equation was clinical depression. Like a gathering storm, it moved into my life the year I turned twenty-four.

At the time, I had no idea what was happening to me—only that the "on fire for Jesus" feeling was suddenly gone, replaced with a range of clouds so thick and dark that I couldn't see past them. I sat in bed with my Bible, my journal, *My Utmost for His Highest*, just like I always had, but the great clouded mass moved closer until I felt myself disappear into it . . . and it felt to me that God had left entirely.

Those were the dark days.

At first, I read the Bible desperately, trying to reignite the flame of my ashen faith, but the promises of God's presence filling the pages felt cruel and untrue to me. Eventually I stopped trying at all. The old, holy words felt wooden, and when I tried to read them they splintered into my heart in the most painful way.

I journaled less and drank more. I avoided Oswald Chambers entirely. His adherence to the holiness movement—a set of beliefs that I now actually understood, thanks to my Bible college's theology classes and its intensely detailed "Lifestyle Statement"—put me on the defensive. I'd grown to resent Chambers's stern certainty, his black-and-white declarations in a world that, for me, had become almost entirely gray.

My Utmost for His Highest: the title itself seemed to mock me. I could not give God my "utmost." All I had was my broken, basement-level self with all its darkness and narcissism and doubt. And I wasn't sure I even wanted to give Him that.

I had kept my end of the bargain, after all. I'd executed the equation perfectly for twenty-four years . . . and yet I had not gotten *more* God. I had longed for holiness; instead, I'd gotten this suffocating silence, this endless dark.

Nearly a decade has passed since that first debilitating introduction to clinical depression. It has never gone away.

There are things that have helped—medication, sunlight, the practice of gratitude, the intentional work of community—but those clouds that rolled in during my early twenties have never entirely dissipated. I suspect they never will.

After nine years, I am familiar with my weather patterns. I can tell when another bad bout of depression is coming the way an arthritic can feel an impending storm in her knees. I am learning how to prepare, how to weather it, but it still knocks me off my feet almost every time it sweeps in, so powerful and absolute.

But mostly, depression is just that gray, clouded tint that always hovers over the landscape of my soul. It is always present but not altogether crushing, and it has changed the topography of my faith over time. It is the constant rain that has formed deep chasms in me, channels that are slowly being filled with a new understanding of God's grace and love. It is the fog that obscures everything I thought I knew about God and instead ushers in wonder and mystery.

I suppose that is what Oswald Chambers meant when he wrote about the clouds.

"In the Bible," he said, "clouds are always connected with God. . . . God cannot come near without clouds, He does not come in clear shining."

A decade ago, I wouldn't have understood. The sentiment would have seemed as trite and blaring as "God won't give you more than you can handle." I would have written off Oswald himself as an unfeeling automaton who couldn't possibly understand.

Except I think now that maybe he did.

After all, Chambers himself seems to have struggled through deeply ominous periods. Though the term isn't used in his biography, one can speculate that he too may have lived with clinical depression. In a testimony he gave about the period of time directly after he asked God for "the baptism of the Holy Spirit, whatever that meant," he said something that I could have written of my own early twenties:

> From that day on for four years, nothing but the overruling grace of God and the kindness of friends kept me out of an asylum. God used me during those years for the conversion of souls, but I had no conscious communion with Him. The Bible was the dullest, most uninteresting book in existence.

It turns out that Chambers had sat exactly where I did—albeit a century earlier—with a Bible that felt leaden, a pen that had run dry of praise, a God who had fallen entirely silent behind the clouded sky.

"It is not true to say that God wants to teach us something in our trials," Chambers says in the July 29 reading. "Through every cloud He brings, He wants us to *unlearn* something."

I am thinking that maybe Chambers isn't being dismissive or sentimental here at all.

I'm thinking that maybe he's right.

I'm thinking about all that I've *unlearned* over the past nine years: the simplified equations, the rote answers, the blind certainties. They were things that looked great on the Christian T-shirts that I liked to buy and the bumper stickers I begged my Dad to let me put on my first car. But, in the end, they were only ever a distraction from the stunning simplicity of faith: "Jesus only."

So I am becoming acquainted with the clouds.

The "clear shining" faith of my youth is gone, and in spite of the nostalgia I sometimes feel for that fiery, passionate person I was, it's a good thing.

I can still see her, standing at the front of the church gymnasium with her high ponytail and her heart on fire. "Holiness is what I long for. Holiness is what I need!" She is singing the words to the worship song with all the certainty in the world . . . but it's taken me all these years of clouds, of unlearning, to realize that it wasn't ever holiness that I was meant to long for.

It was only ever Jesus.

Behold, He cometh with the clouds, and I am learning to be grateful.

The wind blows the clouds in, sweeping so much away,

revealing the empty spaces that I so often cram with that which never fills.

It is making room for the One True Thing that I need. I am being filled up slowly by love, by grace, by *Jesus only, Jesus only, Jesus only.*

Addie Zierman is a writer, blogger, and speaker. She has an MFA from Hamline University and is the author of *Night Driving* and *When We Were On Fire: A Memoir of Consuming Faith, Tangled Love, and Starting Over*, named by *Publishers Weekly* as one of the best books of 2013. Addie has also been published in a variety of magazines and journals. She is a Diet Coke enthusiast with terrible taste in TV and an endless pile of Books-To-Read. She lives in Minnesota with her husband, Andrew, and her two young sons, Dane and Liam.

ALAN PERSONIUS

*Ministering in everyday opportunities
that surround us does not mean that we select
our own surroundings—it means being God's
very special choice to be available for use
in any of the seemingly random surroundings
which He has engineered for us.*
SEPTEMBER 11, "MISSIONARY WEAPONS"
(UPDATED EDITION)

For each generation, in each person's life, there is at least one defining moment from which all other time is referenced. For my grandparents it was December 7, 1941—a date which will live in infamy. They could remember exactly where they were and what they were doing when they learned of the attack on Pearl Harbor. For my parents' generation, it was the assassination of President John F. Kennedy. For baby boomers like myself, our defining moment will always be 9/11.

For me, September 11, 2001, began like many other mornings before it. I was serving as an Army officer on the Headquarters, Department of the Army Staff, and was stationed at the Pentagon in Arlington, Virginia. My early commute usually got me to the office, Room 2D547, before most of the people I worked with. I filled the few quiet moments with Scripture reading and a daily devotional passage from *My Utmost for His Highest* by Oswald Chambers.

When I finished with *My Utmost*, I folded the French flap in like a bookmark to save the page, tossed the book onto my desk, and proceeded to the day's work. What started as a routine day soon took a dramatic turn, however, as the events of 9/11 unfolded.

My office had limited access to the Internet, and no television. We were all stunned by the initial reports of an airplane crashing into the World Trade Center, and assumed it was a just terrible accident. When we heard that a second airliner had hit the Twin Towers, we realized these events were actually part of a deliberate terrorist attack. Just as we comprehended this horrible reality, a tremendous explosion rocked *our* building. We were later to learn it was American Airlines Flight 77 crashing into the western wall of the Pentagon, about a hundred yards from where I stood at the time.

The shock wave knocked me to my knees. The ceiling partially collapsed, light fixtures fell, and a mixture of dust and smoke filled the air. Nobody panicked, but there was confusion and alarm. In spite of what we knew had just happened in New York City, we did not know the cause of this blast. Some thought it might be a construction accident, as the area between our corridor and the next, Corridors 4 and 5, was being renovated.

The nearest exit, at the outer end of Corridor 5, was blocked by debris and smoke, so we turned and went the other direction, toward the open-air courtyard in the center of the Pentagon. We had about a hundred yards to travel.

Some distance ahead, I noticed a woman who seemed to be walking aimlessly, as if in a daze. It looked like her hair was covered with cobwebs, and her face was covered with pink and gray patches. I was a little disoriented myself, and not sure what to think of this. About the time I got next to the woman, three men rushed up to her and provided what help they could.

At that moment I became fully aware of what was happening: the woman's hair wasn't covered in cobwebs, it was melted—singed and mixed with ash. The gray patches on her face were flaps of burned skin, hanging down to reveal the pink flesh underneath. She didn't cry or scream, and I wonder now if her lungs had been seared from inhaling a flash fire. The last I saw of the lady in Corridor 5, she was being well cared for by the three men who had come to her aid.

In the center courtyard, I joined hundreds of other people who had fled the explosion. We could see an enormous plume of black smoke rising from the direction we'd come. Police officers directed us to a tunnel that led us through a different section of the Pentagon and outside the building. As we came into the southwest parking lot, we saw for the first time the extent of the damage. Word spread quickly that it was indeed an airliner that had crashed into the building.

It would be several hours before I could get safely home. I spent a lot of time trying to call my wife, Julie, on my cell phone, and when I finally got through, I had only a few moments of battery power left. It was so good to hear her voice, and for her to hear mine—until that moment, she had no idea that I had survived. Since I was the only person in my group who had grabbed a cell phone as we evacuated, I quickly passed it around so the others could give Julie their contact information before the battery died. She, in turn, called their families to tell them their loved ones were safe.

Two weeks after 9/11, after work crews had cleared away

some of the rubble and stabilized the area, a few of us were escorted into what remained of our old offices. We were to secure sensitive material and salvage any personal items that were worth keeping. When I found my desk, I pushed aside soggy ceiling tiles and other debris and found my copy of *My Utmost for His Highest* just where I had left it. It was water-stained and smelled of smoke. I opened it to the page I had previously marked with the back flap, and noticed a smoke line on the September 11 passage.

Every year since, when I come to that page in my devotional, I'm reminded of my experiences on 9/11. The September 11 entry in the updated edition concludes by saying, "if we do not steadily minister in everyday opportunities, we will do nothing when the crisis comes." That continues the theme from the previous day's reading, stating, "If you are not doing the task that is closest to you now, which God has engineered into your life, when the crisis comes, instead of being fit for battle, you will be revealed as being unfit. Crises always reveal a person's true character." The smoke line in my devotional reminds me to prepare in my everyday opportunities so I will be ready to minister to others in their critical times of need.

One of my favorite authors is C. S. Lewis. In *The Weight of Glory* he writes, "There are no *ordinary* people. You have never talked to a mere mortal. Nations, cultures, arts, civilisations—these are mortal, and their life is to ours as the life of a gnat. But it is immortals whom we joke with, work with, marry, snub, and exploit." We encounter immortals every day, including our family and friends, our neighbors, the person sitting next to us at work, and complete strangers like that woman in Corridor 5. Sometimes it is obvious they are in crisis, while other times we are oblivious to their needs. We who know Christ have the opportunity and the obligation to positively influence whomever we encounter, not a single one a "mere mortal." We are all facing eternity.

I believe that God, by His grace and mercy, provided someone to come on the scene and help that lady in Corridor 5. And I believe that God was also looking out for me. I too have been saved, in more ways than one, by God's grace.

On 9/11, I was saved because my office was not any closer to the impact point. I was also saved because the nearby renovation project was behind schedule. Our office was supposed to have moved into that part of the building—between Corridors 4 and 5—in July 2001. But we had been told that we would have to wait until October to move, and that delay saved my life.

This particular morning was clearly a defining moment for me, but the most significant moment in my life occurred years earlier, when I made the decision to accept Jesus as my Lord and Savior.

I was saved by God's grace, perhaps to be here today to share my story with others—my conviction that how we relate to people in everyday, mundane circumstances can prepare us for crisis times, whether physical or spiritual. The simple, routine priorities we have and the actions we take in our everyday lives define who we are, and how—or if—we will be ready when someone needs us. Our actions in all our encounters and relationships have eternal consequences—because those we impact are no mere mortals.

In the years after 9/11 I earned a seminary degree, retired from the Army, and transitioned into a new career in ministry, and now serve as executive pastor of a church in Colorado Springs, Colorado. If you were to look at my old Army uniform as it hangs in my closet, you would see that I have rank and numerous award ribbons from over twenty-four years of active military service. Each represents a significant event or accomplishment, and they all have a special meaning to me. None, however, are as meaningful as the lesson I learned in the Pentagon's Corridor 5. The events of that fateful day have taught me to "steadily minister in everyday opportunities."

Alan Personius and his wife, Julie, currently live in Colorado Springs, Colorado, where he is the executive pastor of Sunnyside Christian Church. He has earned a B.A. in political science from the University of Minnesota, and an M.A. degree in biblical and theological studies from Grace University in Omaha, Nebraska. In 2009, Alan retired from a twenty-four-year career in the US Army. He and Julie have four children and one grandchild.

JONI EARECKSON TADA

What men call training and preparation,
God calls the end.

JULY 28, "AFTER OBEDIENCE—WHAT?"

Whenever Daddy would build stone walls on our Maryland farm, he wouldn't rush. He would pick up a rock, brush it off, turn it over in his hands, and line it up, placing it "just right" into the wall. He paid attention to what he was doing in each moment. He stayed focused on the task at hand. As a result, seventy years later, the walls haven't crumbled.

My stone-laying father would say that's the only way to live. Dad used to tell me, "Don't grasp for the future, Joni. You have to pay attention to the present." He knew I had a tendency to look beyond the horizon, as though my present responsibilities weren't important enough. Daddy could see that I was mainly killing time, waiting for something more interesting to come my way in life. But you can only shuffle through the present for so long, dreaming about a more exciting future.

That dreaming came to an abrupt halt with the 1967 diving accident in which I became a quadriplegic. Left without use of my hands or legs, I plummeted into depression. My hospital stay was an overwhelming battle to keep my head above water.

After I was released from rehab, I went to live back on our Maryland farm with my sister, Jay. The familiar surroundings were somehow fresh, and I began to seriously consider the lordship of Christ in my life.

Still, I was restless and bored with my life in a wheelchair. I wanted to understand the *real* reasons God allowed my quadriplegia to happen: *Maybe God is preparing me for a big ministry in the future. Perhaps my accident is fitting into some grand scheme in which the Lord can use me in better, more important ways. Or maybe He's allowed all this to happen so He can do a big miracle, healing me and getting everybody's attention!*

My thoughts were all about the future. I was rushing through Bible reading and prayer, eager to learn the lessons I was supposed to learn, all so I could get on with the really "important" ministry. Sitting in a wheelchair on the farm wasn't going to take me anywhere. God could not possibly intend for me to live with the status quo . . . could He? Whenever a new twist of circumstances occurred, I'd automatically think about my future, reasoning that God basically allowed things to happen as preparation for something else down the line.

But one July day in 1971, I sat outside our farmhouse by the stone wall Daddy had built. It was a beautiful summer morning and Jay had set up my music stand in front of me— it held my reading material so I could turn the pages with a mouth stick. On the stand, she had plopped *My Utmost for His Highest.*

I had used this classic devotional when I was in high school, and only recently pulled it off the shelf to reread. As I flipped through the month of July, I stumbled across the reading for July 28, noticing these words from Oswald Chambers:

> What is my dream of God's purpose? His purpose is that I depend on Him and on His power now. If I can stay in the middle of the turmoil calm and unperplexed, that is the end of the purpose of God. God is not working towards a particular finish; His end is the process.

The words were from Chambers, but it sounded like a lesson from my father: "Don't grasp for the future, Joni. You have to pay attention to the present!" It's exactly what Chambers—or, I should say, the Holy Spirit—had been trying to tell me.

I had made the mistake of thinking every circumstance, incident, or issue was God's way of preparing me for future ministry. The present moment didn't count; it was merely an incidental link in a long chain of events leading toward some better thing on the horizon. Although every situation was one more thread in the overall embroidery, details that would fit—as the J. B. Phillips version of the Bible says— "into a pattern for good" (Romans 8:28), I never bothered to look for God's good *right now.*

I stopped and savored the July 28 devotional again. My eyes became wet when I read these words about God's grace for *right now*: "It is the process, not the end, which is glorifying to God. . . . If we realise that obedience is the end, then each moment as it comes is precious."

The process is the end. No wonder I was so restless in my wheelchair, and always battling feelings of discontentment. Oswald Chambers's words revealed my agitation and impatience with my quadriplegia. I didn't like being in it, or learning from it, in the moment—instead, I kept longing for better times in the future.

Looking down at my paralyzed legs, I realized God wanted me to be patient *now*. Learn to accept hardship *now*. And discover a fresh dependency on and intimacy with my Savior *now*. Slowly, over time, the process of my growth in Christ became an end in itself.

Even my prayers began to change. *Jesus,* I would pray, *I don't want to miss your blessings today. If I'm supposed to learn something special today, help me keep my eyes open.* I discovered a delightful happiness in Jesus Christ, right now and for this moment. *This* was God's purpose, even His goal for my life!

And now, decades later, I see that seeking God in the moment has somehow evolved into a global ministry to people with disabilities—as I sought my Savior in the moment, those increments became the chain of events that ultimately resulted in Joni and Friends, a worldwide outreach that reaches thousands of special-needs families for Christ. Still, what is primary in my life is appropriating the grace of God in everything that happens today. In heaven, the Lord will not be excited with how many books I've written or how big an organization I've led. He will be impressed with how I've yielded to His will, submitted to His discipline, and loved His Son, Jesus.

How does this principle work in your life? Let's suppose you don't get accepted into the college of your choice; you wonder how a lesser-known school will affect God's plan for your future. You worry how your career choice could be impacted, or that you might not meet your future husband. But God's purpose may be to test your *response*—will you grumble and complain, or will you willingly submit and trust God with this circumstance? *That's* paying sufficient attention to the immediate.

God's Word is filled with admonitions to "number our

days" (Psalm 90:12) and "make the most of every opportunity" (Ephesians 5:16 NLT). So slow down and live . . . *really* live by keeping in step with the Spirit (Galatians 5:25). Watch for what the Lord wants to teach you in each circumstance in which you find yourself.

In 2017 I will crest fifty years in my wheelchair. I look back and see how each decade is made up of precious conversations, priceless friendships, wise (and sometimes unwise) decisions, and ongoing study and prayer. Each is a treasured link in an amazing chain that has led me to this day. I'm not about to rush through the present moment in order to reach the next one.

Like my daddy would say—like Oswald Chambers said—pay sufficient attention to the *now* in your life. For when the process is the end, you'll see your Savior, enjoy His grace, and relish His pleasure in every delightful moment.

Joni Eareckson Tada is founder and CEO of Joni and Friends, an organization that accelerates Christian outreach in the disability community. Joni and Friends provides practical support and spiritual help to special needs families worldwide. Joni is the author of numerous best-selling books, including *Joni and Ken: An Untold Love Story, Diamonds in the Dust,* and the Gold Medallion Award–winning *When God Weeps.* Joni and her husband, Ken, reside in Calabasas, California. For more information, visit joniandfriends.org.

Take *My Utmost for His Highest* everywhere you go with the *My Utmost for His Highest* app

Enjoy this book? Help us get the word out!

Share a link to the book or
mention it on social media

Write a review on your blog, on
a retailer site, or on dhp.org

Pick up another copy to
share with someone

Recommend this book for your
church, book club, or small group

Follow *My Utmost for His Highest* on
social media and join the discussion

 @MyUtmostForHisHighest 	@myutmost  @myutmost

Contact us to share your thoughts:

Discovery House
P.O. Box 3566
Grand Rapids, MI 49501 USA

1-800-653-8333
books@dhp.org
utmost.org